# RSPB Guide to
# British
# Birds

# RSPB Guide to British Birds

## David Saunders

Illustrated by Noel Cusa

# Hamlyn

London · New York · Sydney · Toronto

Line drawings and flight plates by Peter Hayman

The map of Dipper distribution on page 21 is reproduced by permission of the British Trust for Ornithology/Irish Wildbird Conservancy Atlas Project.

Published by
The Hamlyn Publishing Group Limited
London · New York · Sydney · Toronto
Astronaut House, Feltham, Middlesex, England
Copyright © The Hamlyn Publishing Group Limited 1975
Colour plates copyright © Noel Cusa 1970

ISBN 0 600 33942 4

Phototypeset by Keyspools Limited, Golborne, Lancashire
Printed by Tinling (1973) Limited, Prescot, Merseyside

# Foreword

The *RSPB Guide to British Birds* is intended for beginners, for adults and youngsters who have realized that they want to know the names of birds which they see round their houses and on their holidays. It has one great advantage over other guides: it depicts only 218 species, which is about half of the total number recorded on the British list. Birdwatching is a growing pastime and we hope that this book will lead you deeper into the study of birds, and help you to become a 'curious' naturalist.

Identification is only the first part of real birdwatching. You cannot really learn anything about birds until you know what you are looking at. Once you have reached the stage of being certain about your bird identification, the door is opened to an intriguing world of the lives and habits of birds. You must remember to be inquisitive about what you see. Of course, by merely asking the question 'What bird is that?' you have started on a path of inquisitiveness about nature. Once you have identified your bird and started to observe carefully, and preferably to record in your notebook how the bird is behaving, the next question to ask yourself is 'Why is that bird behaving like that?'

At this point you may rush to one of the books which David Saunders has mentioned to find the answer, or you may try out the question on the lecturer at your evening class—if you have one in your district. You may find it impossible to get an answer to your question and then you are left with the problem that you ought to consider trying to solve it yourself. This entails making repeated observations on how the bird behaves in a variety of situations. You may finish up with more questions than you started with, but you will have given yourself much enjoyment and a lasting hobby.

This book will also help you to enjoy nature in a more contemplative way. To identify a bird is to begin to identify ourselves with our natural environment. To know a creature by name links us with it and we begin to understand its place in nature, and become concerned with what we are doing to the natural environment, without which neither we nor birds can live. To be able to name the birds we see helps us to enjoy nature more, and intensifies the pleasure that the song and beauty of birds can bring us.

I believe that this guide, ably written by David Saunders, will guide us into the beginning of a fascinating and beautiful world.

Peter Conder

Director, Royal Society for the
Protection of Birds

# Preface

I have watched birds for over twenty years, and like most birdwatchers I am continually hoping to see a new species or a more familiar one in a different area, but I still obtain the greatest pleasure in watching and indeed encouraging our more common birds. Some are not as well known as one might have expected. It is these common birds which first awaken our interest, whether as the enthusiastic schoolboy taking up a new hobby, or as so many discover, as an absorbing retirement pastime.

We all soon realize that even in our garden birds will be seen which we cannot name, and the often thorny problem of identification arises. The *RSPB Guide to British Birds* concentrates on those species most likely to be encountered and excludes the many vagrants and wanderers to these islands whose descriptions all too often confuse the beginner. It is designed as an introduction to further information about our common species, and describes how to pursue the hobby of birdwatching.

There is no substitute for field observation, a point which can never be over emphasized, as this is the only real way to study birds and to learn something of them. I therefore hope that this book will prompt many to take the preliminary step on the birdwatching road, with its abundant pleasures and excitements awaiting discovery.

I should like to thank the staff of the RSPB for their advice and assistance during the preparation of this book.

D.S.

# Contents

# Introduction

Feathers are found in no class of animal other than birds, and their structure has changed little since the first birds appeared in Jurassic times, 150 million years ago. Because they are both light and strong, feathers efficiently serve a number of important roles and enable birds to exist in all areas and habitats except those of extreme altitude or low temperature. Contour feathers provide a streamlined outline essential for efficient flight; at the same time their intricate structure and the presence of inner down feathers ensure the provision of innumerable minute air pockets which act as an insulating medium. In cold weather we have all seen birds fluff out their feathers, so achieving a temporary increase in this insulated area. Thus, as long as food can be found, some bird species are able to exist in areas where few other animals can survive.

To keep their feathers in good condition birds preen. Most birds possess an oil or preen gland situated close to the base of the tail on the upperside, the 'parson's nose' of table poultry. It seems most highly developed in aquatic species and although it may serve other functions, its main one would seem to be that of enabling the bird to maintain its plumage in a waterproof condition. Thus, some birds have been able to evolve mainly aquatic habits; some seabirds spend most of their lives at sea, coming ashore only to breed.

The wings, powered by immense pectoral muscles, enable movement through the air to be made with, in most cases, apparent ease. In some larger species prolonged gliding flight is made possible by air currents and up-draughts which keep the birds aloft with very little expenditure of energy. Although flight is by no means restricted to birds it is they above all other groups of animals which have brought it to the peak of perfection. There is nothing to compare the apparent ease with which a Fulmar hangs in the up-draught close to its cliff-ledge nest site, the stoop of a Peregrine after its prey, or the aerial artistry of a group of Swifts as they scream about our rooftops in midsummer.

A few species have lost the ability to fly. Some, like the Ostrich which lives in open country, run in order to escape from danger, while others like the Kiwi have nocturnal or exceedingly retiring habits. Penguins are unable to fly but retain their powerful pectoral muscles for speedy and dexterous underwater propulsion, as did the Great Auk of the North Atlantic. This fine bird unfortunately became extinct during the early nineteenth century as a result of its inability to fly and consequent over-exploitation by man.

Ease of movement, particularly in flight, together with highly developed

Opposite and over page *One example from each of the major families of birds shows the variety to be found within just the birds of Britain.*

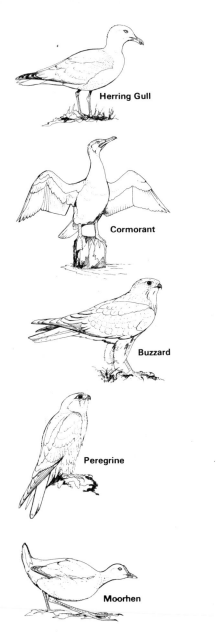

Herring Gull

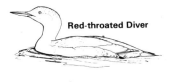

Red-throated Diver

Cormorant

Manx Shearwater

Buzzard

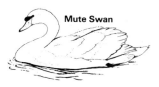

Mute Swan

Peregrine

Red Grouse

Moorhen

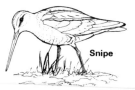

Snipe

9

Puffin

Woodpigeon

Swift

Barn Owl

Raven

Green
Woodpecker

Long-tailed Tit

Goldcrest

Blackbird

House Sparrow

organs for sight and hearing mean that most birds are able to remain relatively conspicuous when compared with mammals. There is less need to remain concealed so that many species have evolved bright plumages. In some the sexes may look alike, in others they differ and males are usually brighter. This may be taken to extremes in a few species with a distinct plumage being developed only for the early part of the breeding season. A good example is the male Ruff, whose extravagant head and neck feathers are used during its flamboyant communal displays.

The size of British birds varies from the Goldcrest at a mere 9 cm ($3\frac{1}{2}$ in) to the Mute Swan at 152 cm (60 in) in length. With their great mobility it is hardly surprising that birds have dispersed widely during their evolution in order to exploit fully every habitat, whether it be for food or for breeding sites. This accounts for the great differences in body size and shape, coloration, flight, swimming and diving abilities, in the shape and use of the bill, and in breeding biology.

Some birds have become sedentary, finding all their requirements within a small area. Others may have to roam more widely out of the breeding season, and many have evolved seasonal migrations which take the birds some thousands of kilometres each year. Thus, in addition to resident species we receive summer and winter visitors, together with those which use these islands simply as staging posts on their great journeys, and are only seen for short periods each autumn and spring.

Such diversification of structure, habits and requirements, together with their bright colours, combine to make birds one of the most intensely watched and studied of all classes of wildlife. By tropical standards our avifauna may be limited; we nevertheless have in these islands a wealth of birds to be enjoyed.

One does not have to go far in order to see a variety of species, indeed no further than our windows, for quite a number visit our gardens and many not normally encountered there may be attracted by the provision of food and water. This is just as possible in cities and towns as it is in the open countryside. City parks are ideal for both birds and their watchers, while there can be few people who do not live within reach of a gravel pit or reservoir. Those able to travel will soon discover that fine estuaries, islands and moorland are all easily accessible, opening up a new range of habitats and the different birds which they support.

# Birdwatching equipment

Although some people enjoy watching birds at close range from their home without a binocular, for the majority this piece of equipment is an essential item. Certainly, on most occasions its use is absolutely necessary if birds are to be correctly identified and their behaviour studied with any accuracy. There is now a great choice of binoculars available with good ones from Japan, Russia and the United States, besides better known makes from both East and West Germany and Great Britain. Prices vary enormously.

By trying out the binoculars of friends and acquaintances when on field trips, it is soon possible to discover the type of model and magnification which most suits your requirements before making a purchase. Another method is to buy on approval from one of the several optical firms which regularly advertise in the bird magazines. Do not rush for extremely high magnifications; these are not an advantage unless combined with equally large and thus expensive object glasses. In fact, disregard models of over 12x magnification and aim preferably for something in the range 7x to 10x.

There is a second figure stamped on the binocular body, as well as the magnification, and this is the object glass diameter, for example, 8 ×40 or 9 ×63. By dividing this figure by the magnification, a factor known as the exit pupil diameter is obtained. The exit pupil diameter is a measure of the light gathering properties of the binocular and of how bright the image will be, and should for preference be not less than 5. Good light gathering qualities really come into their own on dull days or as dusk approaches. Among other points to look for are a convenient weight, clarity of image right across the field of view, and an absence of colour or chromatic aberration which fringes the image.

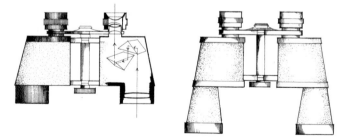

*The diagram of the general purpose, 8 × 40 binocular* (left) *shows how the prism arrangement reflects the light several times. The 10 × 50 binocular* (right) *gives greater magnification but is larger and heavier to handle. Note in both cases the position of the focusing knob. In this position heavier binoculars can be handled more easily.*

An excellent way of attracting birds to close range is by means of a bird table or feeding station. This is normally a tray erected in the garden on a post, or hanging from a tree or even attached to a window ledge. Supplied with a variety of foods, especially in hard weather when natural sources may be frozen or snow covered, it will prove irresistible to many species and be of great interest to the observer. Seeds, kitchen scraps, especially fatty items, nuts and chopped apple (windfalls are excellent) are all readily taken. Half coconuts will be visited endlessly by tits which are also much addicted to peanuts. The latter when offered in red plastic nets seem to be a special attraction to Siskins and these dainty finches are coming increasingly to gardens in many areas.

Do not forget to provide a small shallow pool for drinking purposes. Birds need fresh water right through the year and its provision is a simple matter. In a woodland habitat one observer recorded no less than thirty-three species visiting such a pool as he watched from a nearby hide. In a garden no hide is necessary, the house being the best one possible.

No garden, however small or surrounded by buildings, should be without a nestbox. These come in two basic types along with more specialized designs. That for hole-nesting species is usually erected for use by Great and Blue Tits, though with enlargement and adaptation can be made suitable for owls and woodpeckers. Open-fronted boxes, not quite so readily occupied, may nevertheless be used by birds such as the Robin and Spotted Flycatcher. Several commercial designs are currently advertised, but little skill is required to construct one's own, and this is certainly much cheaper. The main points to remember are not to make the entrance hole too large, 28mm ($1\frac{1}{8}$in) is ample for tits, and to ensure that the box is draught- and damp-proof. The RSPB produces a range of bird garden equipment, including nestboxes and bird tables.

Books are an important item high on any birdwatcher's list of equipment, their choice being made difficult in a pleasing way by the

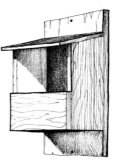

*If erected during winter, the standard tit box* (left) *is usually occupied during early March. Careful siting of the open-fronted box for the Spotted Flycatcher or Robin* (right) *is necessary for success.*

great and ever-increasing number of titles published. They may for convenience be best divided into three categories: identification, information and supplementation, of which the first is the most important, needing at least one representative on all birdwatchers' bookshelves.

## Identification books

Along with binoculars, no birdwatcher should be without an identification book of which there are several equally good ones currently available. Unlike this book, all extend their range beyond the confines of Great Britain and Ireland which means the inclusion of species rarely if ever seen here; something which may cause confusion to the beginner. Most recently published is the *The Birds of Britain and Europe with North Africa and the Middle East* by Heinzel, Fitter and Parslow (1972). Despite the fine illustrations and maps, the wide geographical range means that this is not a book to be purchased in advance of other guides, unless one is rushing off to foreign parts.

Both *The Hamlyn Guide to Birds of Britain and Europe* by Bruun and Singer (1970) and *A Field Guide to the Birds of Britain and Europe* by Peterson, Mountfort and Hollom (revised edition 1974), cover somewhat smaller areas but are also profusely illustrated and contain distribution maps. The former has the better layout—the species description, illustration and map all appearing together. In the latter these items are separated, at times widely, while many of the illustrations are in black and white. On the other hand, identification is greatly assisted by means of the Peterson system of indicator lines which draw attention to the major diagnostic features of each species.

One word of warning concerning all field guides; as their very name suggests they are *guides* to identification, so do not think one simply has to open them and hey-presto that mysterious bird on the lawn can immediately be named. Many other factors combine to aid identification and not infrequently to hinder it. Observation conditions, binocular and telescope used, other species with which the bird might be confused, and the watcher's own skill all play a part. The correct use of a field guide is just one part of a sometimes lengthy process. The number of species packed into the small volumes mentioned is in itself a drawback as normally only the main plumage of each is illustrated, while the text is of necessity of the briefest nature. Always bear these facts in mind when reaching for the field guide; it is an invaluable tool but must never become the master. There is no substitute for the experience gained by many hours of observation in the field.

Of a more specialized nature was the publication in 1974 of a book *Flight Identification of European Raptors* by Porter, Willis, Christensen and Nielsen. This, one hopes, marks the start of a new trend in identification; the detailed study of small groups of birds which raise special problems for the observer. Certainly there are some groups, among them seabirds and waders, for which similar specialized works are long overdue. One hopes that industrious birdwatchers are already working on such projects for which the need is real.

## Information books

Books providing information about birds and birdwatching are legion. Some are of the most general nature; others amass vast quantities of knowledge concerning a single species or an aspect of bird biology. A number tell the beginner how to set about birdwatching and so join the now countless others who have adopted this most enjoyable pastime.

Among the first of these latter books was *Watching Birds* by James Fisher, published as a Penguin in 1940. Now, over thirty years later, it has been extensively revised and reissued in hard covers. It is a pity that its price puts this invaluable work beyond the reach of many beginners, especially children. For a more modest amount *Birdwatching* by Saunders, published in 1975 by Hamlyn in their all-colour paperbacks series, is good value. *Birds* by Christopher Perrins introduces the subject of bird ecology—the study of how birds have successfully adapted to life in various habitats—and is also recommended.

Several books on particular techniques have appeared, photography with many devotees being one. Both *An Introduction to Bird and Wildlife Photography* by Marchington and Clay (1974), and *Wildlife Photography* by Gooders and Hosking (1973), should be consulted by anyone wishing to enlarge their interests to include the photography of birds. Most of us begin our watching in the garden and even the most experienced will find the *The New Bird Table Book* by Soper (1973) a compendium of information. The invaluable series of low-priced booklets published by the British Trust for Ornithology are excellent value and include *Nestboxes* (BTO Guide 3), *Binoculars, Telescopes and Cameras* (BTO Guide 14), and *Bird Ringing* (BTO Guide 16).

County avifauna lists are a source of valuable information concerning the local distribution of birds and their numbers. A study of the relevant work will be most helpful in planning birdwatching excursions. Some counties are better endowed than others and among the most recently published are *A Guide to the Birds of Essex* by Hudson and Pyman (1968), *Birds of Devon* by Moore (1969), and *A Revised List of Hampshire and Isle of Wight Birds* by Cohen and Taverner (1972). A recent though growing innovation is the publication of brief guides to specific areas like the Shetlands, Pennines, Pembrokeshire and Exmoor; these are usually low priced but contain a wealth of background information.

The ornithologist may also draw on the rich store of knowledge embodied in the species monographs and books dealing with groups of birds. Two of the undoubted classics in this field are *The Herring Gull's World* by Tinbergen (revised edition 1971) and *Swifts in a Tower* by Lack (revised edition 1973). Other outstanding volumes include *The Fulmar* by Fisher (1952), *The Dotterel* by Nethersole-Thompson (1973), and *The*

*Buzzard* by Tubbs (1974). Several of the books dealing with groups of birds merit attention and include *Woodland Birds* by Simms (1971), *Finches* by Newton (1973) and *The Seabirds of Britain and Ireland* by Cramp, Bourne and Saunders (1974).

## Supplementary books

I place in this category books relating to a birdwatcher's experiences whether in this country or further afield. From these one can often learn much relating to observation techniques and above all to the birds themselves. Recently published titles have included *Birdwatchers' Year* by Batten et al. (1973), *At the Turn of the Tide* by Perry (revised edition 1973), *Seventy Years of Birdwatching* by Alexander (1974) and *The Bird Watchers' Book* edited by John Gooders (1974). Although it is far better to establish one's selection of bird books, cost will be a limiting factor. Most public libraries have good selections, however, and are usually pleased to receive requests for titles not currently on their shelves.

## Sound recordings

Like the field guides, recordings of bird song are an invaluable aid to identification, though every effort must also be made to learn the voices of birds in the field. Few observers will not own or have access to a record player, and if this is the case a selection of records should be obtained. Some records deal with the birds of a certain habitat or area like the BBC Wildlife Recording Series. Others are more wide ranging, though to cover most species the RSPB's seven-inch *Listen the Birds* series requires no less than eighteen records but is excellent value. Cassettes of bird song are also available.

# Identification and the taking of notes

The behaviour and habits of a bird are full of interest but I do not think anyone will deny that the first essential is to be able to name the bird that you are watching. Some are easy to identify; the Magpie and House Sparrow are so well known that they cause no confusion. It will not be long, however, before an unfamiliar species will be met. By following the proper procedure, identification may be attempted and with care prove successful. It will soon become apparent that not all such efforts will be conclusive; dead ends will be reached and the bird remain a mystery, while every care must be taken to avoid errors.

The habit of taking notes should be developed at an early stage of one's birdwatching career, for example, notes of species, numbers, locations, and above all plumage and behaviour descriptions. Such items are essential if correct identifications of a high standard are to be achieved, and this must be the aim of all birdwatchers. When confronted by an apparently new bird, on no account whatsoever should a field guide be consulted as a first step; this should wait until full details have been gathered. It is all too easy to mislead oneself by hurriedly consulting a book before completing the observations of the bird in question.

Plumage details form the bulk of one's notes. On occasions the opportunity will permit these to be made in some detail; on others they will be scanty, the bird moving quickly out of sight and not retraced. Whatever the situation one should relate the information to the named exterior features of the bird. These are depicted in the introductory chapters to all good field guides (in this guide on page 27) and in the various guides to birdwatching, and should be learned. By referring to such parts as the crown, nape, rump, primaries, and so on, the description taken will be easy to compare with those in books, and will facilitate consultation with experts when this is required.

When a strange bird is observed, study it carefully making a mental note of all salient features, for it may disappear quickly. Then transfer this information immediately into the notebook; if the bird conveniently remains in view each item can be checked and when necessary expanded as the observations proceed. Never wait until you return home to write up such notes, do it immediately in the field. If more than one person is present, it is far better for each to make independent notes, a much more desirable method than a single joint effort. One may notice a feature the other missed, while two or more descriptions will confirm and amplify the observations, and considerably assist a correct identification.

Besides the all-important plumage details there are other aspects of the bird which need to be considered in order to arrive at the right conclusion. Size is chief among these, though it is difficult to assess even at close range. Whenever possible compare the unknown bird with familiar species which happen to be in the vicinity; similar comparisons can be made when the field guide is consulted.

The shape and posture of the bird should be noted and can be made more meaningful by once again drawing comparisons with known species. Has it a tall upright stance or a more horizontal posture? How does it move when on the ground or on the water. How does it fly? The method of feeding and the type of food taken are further useful features. Sketches, however rough, can often greatly assist the written description. Not so easily described are details of call notes and song, but these may be critical in the identification procedure and should not be neglected.

# Bird songs and calls

The songs and calls of birds are as diverse as the species from which they originate. It is in the breeding season that the intensity of song reaches a peak, but there is no period in any habitat when birds may not be heard. Birds have developed the means of communication by sounds to a higher degree than any other animal (apart from man), and these are for the most part readily audible and pleasing to the human ear. There are few species which may be considered completely silent but among British species the Shag is rarely heard. One or two birds communicate by non-vocal sounds; the rapid 'drumming' of woodpeckers on the trunks and branches of trees is one example, and the curious sound produced by the tail feathers of Snipe in aerial display, also called 'drumming', is another.

Voice communication in birds takes two basic forms — a song and call notes. Song is most highly developed in the order Passeriformes, or perching species, which comprise most of the world's birds. Here it is used mainly for the establishment and defence of a nesting territory, the attraction of a mate to that territory, and notice to possible rivals that the area is already occupied. Call notes are of value in a variety of situations. They may act as an alarm signal when danger threatens to keep members of a flock together, to intimidate enemies, and as a signal to others when food is sighted.

Most birds have distinctive voices and by becoming familiar with these one has a valuable technique without which some skulking and nocturnal species would perhaps remain unidentified. Bird songs and calls often reveal the presence of such species long before they are observed, especially in such habitats as woodland and reedbed. Many of the Firecrests now breeding in southern England were first located by their characteristic song, and in at least some cases would have been otherwise overlooked. Some species with similar plumage can be safely separated in the field only by voice; for example, the Marsh Tit and Willow Tit, and the Willow Warbler and Chiffchaff.

Bird song has fascinated and moved man throughout the ages, perhaps the song of no species more so than the Nightingale, heard at its best from about mid-April until June. It sings as much by day as during the hours of darkness, though unfortunately it is regularly encountered only in southern districts. Not so the Wren, one of our most widely distributed species; encountered in most habitats, its loud and vigorous song output is quite prodigious for such a small bird.

The bubbling call of the Curlew heard at its breeding grounds is among the most musical sounds produced by larger species, many of which tend to have harsh voices, or only the briefest of songs. The strident calls of the Black-headed Gull nevertheless retain their magic, raucous though they may be. Each note is used by the bird as an important means of communication which, when combined with head and body postures at the breeding ground, is a positive means of identification for paired birds.

Thus, not only is it important for the birdwatcher to learn to identify birds by plumage and voice details, but every endeavour should also be made to discover the meaning of each call. The individual calls carry their own particular messages and patient watching and listening during many long hours in the field are necessary to learn these.

As one's knowledge grows so does the ability to locate birds quickly and accurately, to identify them correctly, and to interpret their actions and behaviour. A clearer understanding of the bird and its behaviour will make one's birdwatching so much more interesting.

*Contrasts in bird calls and song. The call of the Curlew is a pleasant musical bubbling while the Black-headed Gull utters harsh cries. The Wren's song is very loud and strident whereas the Nightingale's is full of rich and varied phrases.*

# Taking your birdwatching further

As so many have found, the pleasures from birdwatching may be increased as one becomes more involved in the hobby. This can take many forms, often leading the birdwatcher towards making contributions to the well-being of the birds themselves, besides obtaining greater pleasure from them.

A way of extending one's interest is to join a birdwatching club or society. This enables contact to be made with other devotees, participation in both indoor meetings and field excursions, and an opportunity of receiving the club journal, bulletin or newsletter. There are several national organizations besides the local ones, together with specialist societies like The Wildfowl Trust, Slimbridge, Gloucester, and the Seabird Group, c/o the Royal Society for the Protection of Birds, The Lodge, Sandy, Beds, SG19 2DL.

Members of the Royal Society for the Protection of Birds receive the bimonthly informative magazine *Birds* which keeps them in touch with conservation matters, developments at reserves, together with more general information concerning birds. The RSPB also has an expanding network of members' groups organizing their own programmes of meetings, film shows and excursions. The Young Ornithologists' Club is also based at Sandy and has its own colour magazine *Bird Life*.

In Scotland, the Scottish Ornithologists' Club, 21 Regent Terrace, Edinburgh EH7 5BT, has active branches in all main centres and publishes *Scottish Birds*. A similar situation has developed in Ireland under the aegis of the Irish Wildbird Conservancy, c/o Royal Irish Academy, 19 Dawson Street, Dublin, which manages a number of important ornithological sites in the Republic as reserves. Throughout England and Wales no area is without a birdwatchers' society of one form or another. Enquiry at your local library or a letter (enclose a stamped and addressed envelope) to the Council for Nature, Zoological Gardens, Regent's Park, London NW1, will soon put you in touch.

The British Trust for Ornithology, Beech Grove, Tring, Hertfordshire, is the main fact-finding organization concerning birds in Great Britain and Ireland. Through its membership, together with other volunteers, it organizes surveys and enquiries, mostly concerning the distribution and numbers of birds, and the factors causing change. Such facts are needed before one can embark upon conservation programmes, or assess what effect alterations to a habitat will have on its bird population. Some of the enquiries are long term, such as those concerning the Great Crested Grebe and Heron. The *Birds of Estuaries Enquiry* mounted by the BTO, RSPB and Wilfowl Trust, has produced invaluable evidence of the importance of our estuaries not only to local birds but also to those from the whole of north-west Europe and parts of the arctic. Between 1968 and 1972 the BTO was engaged upon the *Atlas of Breeding Birds* by which

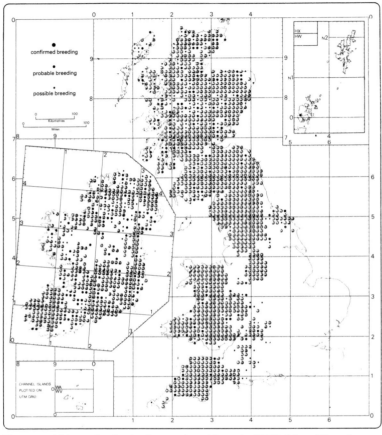

*The map of Dipper distribution is reproduced from the BTO's* Atlas of Breeding Birds *survey and is an example of the valuable results obtainable from cooperative voluntary effort.*

the distribution of all the species of birds breeding in Great Britain and Ireland was plotted on the basis of ten kilometre squares of the National Grid. Surveys currently in progress include a *Register of Ornithological Sites* and a *Waterways Bird Survey,* while in a mammoth operation in 1975 nearly all our rookeries were counted, for the first time since 1945.

For such enquiries as these and those of other organizations, like the Wildfowl Counts of the Wildfowl Trust and the *Beached Birds Survey* of the RSPB, there is a continual need to have more volunteer helpers. Only by ensuring full and accurate coverage, something requiring many observers, can the best information be obtained. This may not be too difficult in southern areas but is something more difficult to arrange in isolated parts, though people on holiday and even special expeditions are used, as occurred during the breeding seabirds survey *Operation Seafarer* mounted by the Seabird Group in 1969–70. Thus, there are many opportunities for the birdwatcher to participate in a variety of important projects ultimately to the benefit of the birds themselves.

Besides cooperative surveys and enquiries, projects of a more restricted nature may be embarked upon to the enjoyment of the investigator. Careful noting of one's observations during these enquiries can often prove of interest and value to others when submitted as a note or paper to one of the ornithological journals. Many ideas for simple fieldwork are given in the book *Projects with Birds* by Goodfellow (1973), and these will suggest other avenues to be explored.

Local surveys can be of value and are probably the best method of really getting to know an area and its birds. Certainly it will ensure a visit to that odd corner, perhaps an isolated copse or neglected pond, that might otherwise be passed by. Spots like these often hold surprises, possibly a species one had not expected. Never miss an opportunity for investigation.

The food of birds is always of interest. Different items can be offered at the bird table and the preferences of each species noted. Birds can also be watched feeding on natural as distinct from provided foods, though here extreme care is necessary to ensure that you really can see what the bird is eating, and not just assume it must be a particular item from the bird's behaviour. The reaction of birds to models or mounted specimens of other birds is something that can be accomplished in most gardens, and will provide insight into the behaviour of birds towards one another.

# Conservation of birds

A variety of factors influences the distribution of birds and possibly the most important at present is that of human activity. At an ever-increasing rate we are exerting pressures on the countryside, and these are decisively moulding our avifauna. Drainage, tree-felling, afforestation, mechanization of agriculture, industrialization, and a greater mobility of the population, including birdwatchers, hold the key to the distribution of many species and their future prospects.

Some birds readily adapt. Many suburban garden species are of woodland origin but now thrive, some even in the inner urban zone. Among seabirds the gulls are great opportunists both in terms of food supply and of nesting sites. Many coastal towns now have roof-nesting Herring Gulls but other species are unable to alter their requirements so easily. The Little Tern nests mainly on open beaches from which it is reluctant to move, even in the face of almost intolerable disturbance. Birds of the wetlands, in particular large reedbeds, have suffered a great diminution in numbers, in some cases to complete extinction as a breeding species in this country as such places have been drained. Changes in our woodlands, felling of broad-leaved trees and replacement by conifers may be disastrous to some birds but tolerated, even approved, by others that extend their range in consequence.

As birds have become rarer so their value to the egg and skin collectors increases, and it is often the activities of such unscrupulous people which have hastened the demise of many species. This was a major threat to many birds in the Victorian era but unfortunately our rare birds still have to face these dangers, and some would have long since vanished were it not for vigilant guardians such as the RSPB.

It is only by retaining and maintaining examples of particularly vulnerable habitats as nature reserves that we can ensure the continued existence as breeding birds of species with specialized requirements in these islands. Reserves must be managed and this is not just a matter of providing a warden and hides, but requires carefully prepared long-term management plans by which the areas can be managed, and where improvements are carried out with a view to making the site even more attractive to birds than it was previously.

Foremost among the voluntary organizations involved with conservation is the Royal Society for the Protection of Birds, founded in 1889. With its headquarters at The Lodge, Sandy, Bedfordshire, and six regional offices, the RSPB now has a staff of nearly 200. The society owns or manages over fifty-six reserves which range in size from Morecambe Bay, Lancashire, to small remote islands like the Ramna Stacks, Shetland, and Grassholm, Pembrokeshire. Some reserves are established to provide protection for a certain endangered species, while others containing a rich variety of habitats provide a sanctuary area for many.

Conservation is not simply the buying or leasing of land as nature reserves for rare species, however. There is much to be done in the field of education, of both young and old. An even more enlightened and responsible public opinion must exist to provide a better future for all birds in these islands. Several of the reserves like those at Rye House Marsh, Hertfordshire, and Vane Farm, Loch Leven, Tayside, are used to a large extent as educational nature centres.

Mention must also be made of the Young Ornithologists' Club for members up to the age of fifteen years, and student membership of the RSPB for those between fifteen and eighteen years. Each year members of

Orkney
Orkney Moorland
Hobbister
Copinsay

Shetland
Ramna Stacks
Fetlar
Noss

Handa
Balranald
Loch of Strathbeg
Loch Garten
Insh Marshes
Vane Farm
Forth Islands
Inchmickery
Horse Island
Coquet Island
Portglenone
Swan Island
Cowpen Marsh
Shanes Castle
Castle Caldwell
St Bees Head
Morecambe Bay
Leighton Moss
Bempton Cliffs
Hornsea Mere
Blacktoft Sands
East Wood
Coombes Valley
Titchwell
Snettisham
Ouse Washes
Ynys-hir
Minsmere
North Warren
The Gwenffrwd
The Lodge
Havergate
Nagshead
Ramsey
Church Wood
Rye House Marsh
Grassholm
Northward Hill
Barfold Copse
Chapel Wood
Dungeness
Arne

these groups have opportunities to join a large programme of week-long courses, mostly based on Youth Hostels, which are organized in many different counties, local activity schemes and nationwide projects.

Birds have undoubtedly benefited from the growing number who obtain enjoyment by watching them, but there are problems. Enthusiasm must be properly controlled and the simple but important rules of the Country Code adhered to. One must always ensure that the welfare of the bird is paramount. If it cannot be seen wait patiently or move on, without creating excessive disturbance in order to flush the bird from cover. This is particularly important where tired migrants are concerned. Simple field-craft at places like estuaries and gravel pits will ensure that waders and wildfowl are not panicked into unnecessary flight. Care and consideration for birds and land-owners must at all times be foremost in the birdwatcher's mind.

Birdwatchers should become acquainted with the law as it relates to birds. Sooner or later someone shooting or even egg collecting will be encountered and a knowledge of the law will be a considerable advantage. All birds and their eggs are protected under the Protection of Birds Act 1954, with amendments in 1967, except for gamebirds which include certain species of duck and wader which may be taken outside the breeding season, and certain pest species which may be killed by an authorized person. The gamebirds and pest species are listed in schedules at the end of the Act.

Certain species, mostly rare breeding birds, or those whose future gives some cause for concern, are listed and are protected by special penalties at all times. This includes wilful disturbance, so even approaching a nest will constitute an offence. In order to examine or photograph one of these species at the nest, a permit is required from the Natural Environment Research Council. Although many specially protected birds are very rare or confined to small areas, several like the Sparrowhawk and Kingfisher, are more widespread.

If at any time you come across an instance of the Protection of Birds Act being broken, contact the police as soon as possible and also the nearest RSPCA Inspector and the headquarters of RSPB. At the same time give full details of the offence, being quite sure of the identity of the bird or birds involved, together with a description of the person committing it (a car number is especially helpful). A most useful booklet *Wild Birds and the Law* is published by the RSPB who will send a copy on the receipt of a first class stamp. It should be in the pocket of every birdwatcher.

Opposite *RSPB reserves in Great Britain and Northern Ireland.*

# How to use this book

The arrangement of birds in the following sections is that given in *A Species List of British and Irish Birds* (BTO Guide 13) (1971). This is the sequence most widely used in Great Britain and Ireland since the adoption in 1952 of the *Check List of the Birds of Great Britain and Ireland*. Commencing with the divers it progresses through the orders until the Passeriformes, the largest order and most advanced birds of all, are reached, concluding with the Tree Sparrow. (There are two exceptions; for the convenience of arranging the plates, the Fulmar is placed with the auks on pages 90 and 91, and for ease of comparison of the females the Pintail and Shoveler have been placed with the Mallard and Gadwall.)

It was not intended that each of the 480 or so species now admitted to the British list should be dealt with in this book. Only those regularly seen in these islands, and which a birdwatcher who is reasonably mobile can expect to see in the course of a season or two's work without much difficulty, are included. Thus, the number illustrated and described totals 218. These may be loosely fitted into five categories, indicated by the coloured borders to the pages, which are as follows: **ducks, geese and swans** (green); **birds of prey and owls** (red); **seabirds** (dark blue); **water birds including herons, rails and waders** (light blue); and **land birds, including some non-passerines** (brown).

Each of the species described is illustrated in colour on the opposite page, and where necessary in flight, the latter as a black and white illustration. Such flight pictures are especially important for difficult groups of birds like waders and wildfowl.

The description of each species has perforce needed to be brief, the total amount of information given depending on the number described on each page. Thus, only the major features are mentioned, mostly under the general headings of flight, voice, habitat and distribution.

In the check list on pages 30 to 33 all the birds now on the British and Irish List are given. For those described in the main body of this book the relevant page number is given. Others omitted from this are placed in one of the following categories:

**AO** resident or visitor of annual occurrence in small numbers, most not breeding in Great Britain and Ireland;

**W** wanderer, seen here in extremely small numbers or only very occasionally;

**V** vagrant with less than twenty occurrences, though several of the species were once seen more frequently;

**E** escaped, liberated or assisted passage birds not unknown; genuine immigrants cannot be separated from these. In some cases small breeding populations have become established in the wild state.

# The exterior features of the bird

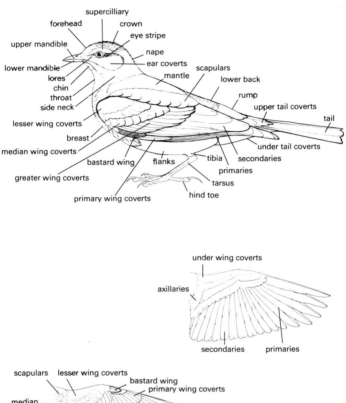

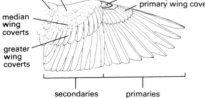

# A short glossary

**Adult** an individual capable of breeding; usually has distinguishing plumage from younger birds

**Axillaries** the feathers of the wingpit

**Carpal joint** the 'wrist' of the bird comprising the forward pointing area on the closed wing

**Colour phase** genetically determined difference in plumage colour within one species. Two or occasionally more distinct colour phases occur in a few species, sometimes with intermediates

**Contour feathers** feathers which cover the body and which provide the streamlined form and retain body heat

**Crepuscular** active only at dusk and dawn

**Crown** upperparts of the head

**Ear coverts** area immediately behind the eye

**Escape** the term given to a bird, perhaps genuinely wild, known to have escaped or been genuinely liberated from captivity

**First year** the period from a bird leaving the nest until the following breeding season

**Hood** where a distinctive colour covers a major part of the head

**Immature** usually denoting a bird from a period after leaving the nest (see also juvenile) until it is able to breed. This may be less than a year, but in longer-lived species will be several and in some cases of up to seven years duration. Immatures are often, but not always, recognizable by a distinctive plumage

**Invasion** when birds normally not or only infrequently seen here arrive suddenly in large numbers

**Juvenile** the period immediately after leaving the nest (see also immature). Division between juvenile and immature is arbitrary

**Mantle** the back feathers and immediately adjoining areas, often all of the same general colour

**Migration** the movement of a bird population from one area to another, frequenting one for breeding and the other for wintering. There are many degrees of migration from the trans-equatorial to merely local movements within our own country

**Nape** upper part of back of neck

**Nostril** opening at each side of the base of the upper mandible

**Passage migrant** a bird not normally breeding or wintering here but regularly seen on migration

**Passeriformes** the largest order of birds, often referred to as the perching birds

**Pectoral muscles** the large muscles of the breast; attached to the sternum or breast bone they provide the strong wing movements necessary for flight

**Pelagic** the deep sea or oceanic habitat, the avifauna of which rarely comes in sight of land except when breeding

**Preen gland** the oil gland which most birds have and which is situated on the rump

**Primaries** the largest and main flight feathers, attached to the 'hand'

**Race** often referred to as the subspecies. Birds of a race may be distinguished from other races of the same species and are normally separated from them geographically. If brought together they can interbreed, the offspring being fertile

**Raptor** another term for bird of prey but excluding owls

**Resident** one found within a given area throughout the year, though some members of the population will disperse and even make local movements

**Rump** the area of the lower back and base of the tail

**Secondaries** the flight feathers of the wing carried on the 'forearm'

**Speculum** a distinctive area of colour in the wing, most often in ducks

**Summer visitor** a bird breeding in this country but absent in winter. Summer being used in the widest sense with some species arriving in March and not leaving until early November

**Territory** any defended area, mostly for breeding purposes though a few species, best known being the Robin, maintain a winter territory

**Winter visitor** birds not normally breeding in this country. Often the first arrive in September with some remaining until early April

# Check list of birds recorded in Great Britain and Ireland

The page reference for species described and illustrated in this book is given; the status of the rest is given according to the key on page 26.

Black-throated Diver *Gavia arctica* 34
Great Northern Diver *G. immer* 34
White-billed Diver *G. adamsii* V
Red-throated Diver *G. stellata* 34
Great Crested Grebe *Podiceps cristatus* 36
Red-necked Grebe *P. grisegena* 36
Slavonian Grebe *P. auritus* 36
Black-necked Grebe *P. nigricollis* 36
Little Grebe *Tachybaptus ruficollis* 36
Pied-billed Grebe *Podilymbus podiceps* V
Black-browed Albatross *Diomedea melanophris* W
Fulmar *Fulmarus glacialis* 90
Capped Petrel *Pterodroma hasitata* V
Bulwer's Petrel *Bulweria bulwerii* V
Cory's Shearwater *Calonectris diomedea* AO
Manx Shearwater *Puffinus puffinus* 38
Little Shearwater *P. assimilis* V
Great Shearwater *P. gravis* AO
Sooty Shearwater *P. griseus* AO
Wilson's Petrel *Oceanites oceanicus* V
Frigate Petrel *Pelagodroma marina* V
Storm Petrel *Hydrobates pelagicus* RV
Leach's Storm Petrel *Oceanodroma leucorhoa* AO
Madeiran Petrel *O. castro* V
Gannet *Sula bassana* 38
Cormorant *Phalacrocorax carbo* 38
Shag *P. aristotelis* 38
White Pelican *Pelecanus onocrotalus* E
Magnificent Frigatebird *Fregata magnificens* V
Grey Heron *Ardea cinerea* 40
Purple Heron *A. purpurea* V
Little Egret *Egretta garzetta* AO
Great White Egret *E. alba* V
Squacco Heron *Ardeola ralloides* W
Cattle Egret *Bubulcus ibis* V
Green Heron *Butorides virescens* V
Night Heron *Nycticorax nycticorax* AO
Little Bittern *Ixobrychus minutus* AO
Bittern *Botaurus stellaris* 40
American Bittern *B. lentiginosus* W
White Stork *Ciconia ciconia* W
Black Stork *C. nigra* V
Spoonbill *Platalea leucorodia* 40
Glossy Ibis *Plegadis falcinellus* W
Greater Flamingo *Phoenicopterus ruber* E
Mallard *Anas platyrhynchos* 42
Black Duck *A. rubripes* V
Teal *A. crecca* 44
Garganey *A. querquedula* 44
Blue-winged Teal *A. discors* W
Baikal Teal *A. formosa* E
Gadwall *A. strepera* 42
Wigeon *A. penelope* 44

American Wigeon *A. americana* W
Pintail *A. acuta* 42
Shoveler *A. clypeata* 42
Wood Duck *Aix sponsa* E
Mandarin Duck *A. galericulata* AO
Red-crested Pochard *Netta rufina* AO
Scaup *Aythya marila* 44
Tufted Duck *A. fuligula* 44
Ring-necked Duck *A. collaris* V
Pochard *A. ferina* 46
Ferruginous Duck *A. nycora* AO
Bufflehead *Bucephala albeola* V
Goldeneye *B. clangula* 46
Long-tailed Duck *Clangula hyemalis* 46
Velvet Scoter *Melanitta fusca* AO
Surf Scoter *M. perspicillata* W
Common Scoter *M. nigra* 46
Harlequin Duck *Histrionicus histrionicus* V
Steller's Eider *Polysticta stelleri* V
Eider *Somateria mollissima* 48
King Eider *S. spectabilis* W
Ruddy Duck *Oxyura jamaicensis* AO
Red-breasted Merganser *Mergus serrator* 48
Goosander *M. merganser* 48
Smew *M. albellus* 48
Hooded Merganser *M. cucullatus* V
Shelduck *Tadorna tadorna* 48
Ruddy Shelduck *T. ferruginea* W
Egyptian Goose *Alopochen aegyptiaca* AO
Greylag Goose *Anser anser* 50
White-fronted Goose *A. albifrons* 50
Lesser White-fronted Goose *A. erythropus* AO
Bean Goose *A. fabalis* 50
Pink-footed Goose *A. brachyrhynchus* 50
Snow Goose *A. caerulescens* W
Brent Goose *Branta bernicla* 52
Barnacle Goose *B. leucopsis* 52
Canada Goose *B. canadensis* 52
Red-breasted Goose *B. ruficollis* W
Mute Swan *Cygnus olor* 52
Whooper Swan *C. cygnus* 52
Bewick's Swan *C. bewickii* 52
Egyptian Vulture *Neophron percnopterus* V
Griffon Vulture *Gyps fulvus* V
Golden Eagle *Aquila chrysaetos* 56
Spotted Eagle *A. clanga* V
Buzzard *Buteo buteo* 56
Rough-legged Buzzard *B. lagopus* AO
Sparrowhawk *Accipiter nisus* 56
Goshawk *A. gentilis* AO
Red Kite *Milvus milvus* 56
Black Kite *M. migrans* V
White-tailed Eagle *Haliaeetus albicilla* V
Honey Buzzard *Pernis apivorus* AO
Marsh Harrier *Circus aeruginosus* 58
Hen Harrier *C. cyaneus* 58
Pallid Harrier *C. macrourus* V
Montagu's Harrier *C. pygargus* 58
Osprey *Pandion haliaetus* 58
Hobby *Falco subbuteo* 60

Peregrine *F. peregrinus* 60
Gyrfalcon *F. rusticolus* AO
Merlin *F. columbarius* 60
Red-footed Falcon *F. vespertinus* AO
Lesser Kestrel *F. naumanni* V
Kestrel *F. tinnunculus* 60
Red Grouse *Lagopus lagopus* 64
Ptarmigan *L. mutus* 64
Black Grouse *Lyrurus tetrix* 64
Capercaillie *Tetrao urogallus* 64
Red-legged Partridge *Alectoris rufa* 66
Grey Partridge *Perdix perdix* 66
Bob-white Quail *Colinus virginianus* E
Quail *Coturnix coturnix* 66
Pheasant *Phasianus colchicus* 66
Golden Pheasant *Chrysolopus pictus* AO
Lady Amherst's Pheasant *C. amherstiae* AO
Reeve's Pheasant *Syrmaticus reevesi* E
Crane *Grus grus* AO
Sandhill Crane *Grus canadensis* V
Water Rail *Rallus aquaticus* 68
Spotted Crake *Porzana porzana* AO
Sora Rail *P. carolina* V
Baillon's Crake *P. pusilla* W
Little Crake *P. parva* W
Corncrake *Crex crex* 68
Moorhen *Gallinula chloropus* 68
Allen's Gallinule *Porphyrula alleni* V
American Purple Gallinule *P. martinica* V
Coot *Fulica atra* 68
Great Bustard *Otis tarda* V
Little Bustard *O. tetrax* W
Houbara Bustard *Chlamydotis undulata* V
Oystercatcher *Haematopus ostralegus* 70
Sociable Plover *Vanellus gregarius* V
Lapwing *V. vanellus* 70
Ringed Plover *Charadrius hiaticula* 70
Little Ringed Plover *C. dubius* 70
Kentish Plover *C. alexandrinus* AO
Killdeer *C. vociferus* V
Caspian Plover *C. asiaticus* V
Grey Plover *Pluvialis squatarola* 70
Golden Plover *P. apricaria* 70
Lesser Golden Plover *P. dominica* V
Dotterel *Eudromias morinellus* 72
Turnstone *Arenaria interpres* 72
Short-billed Dowitcher *Limnodromus griseus* V
Long-billed Dowitcher *L. scolopaceus* V
Stilt Sandpiper *Micropalama himantopus* V
Snipe *Gallinago gallinago* 72
Great Snipe *G. media* W
Jack Snipe *Lymnocryptes minimus* 72
Woodcock *Scolopax rusticola* 72
Upland Sandpiper *Bartramia longicauda* W
Curlew *Numenius arquata* 74
Whimbrel *N. phaeopus* 74
Eskimo Curlew *N. borealis* V
Black-tailed Godwit *Limosa limosa* 74
Bar-tailed Godwit *L. lapponica* 74
Green Sandpiper *Tringa ochropus* 76
Wood Sandpiper *T. glareola* 76
Solitary Sandpiper *T. solitaria* V
Common Sandpiper *T. hypoleucos* 76
Spotted Sandpiper *T. macularia* V
Redshank *T. totanus* 76

Spotted Redshank *T. erythropus* 76
Greater Yellowlegs *T. melanoleuca* V
Lesser Yellowlegs *T. flavipes* W
Greenshank *T. nebularia* 76
Marsh Sandpiper *T. stagnatilis* V
Terek Sandpiper *Xenus cinereus* V
Knot *Calidris canutus* 78
Purple Sandpiper *C. maritima* 78
Little Stint *C. minuta* 78
Least Sandpiper *C. minutilla* V
Temminck's Stint *C. temminckii* AO
Baird's Sandpiper *C. bairdii* W
White-rumped Sandpiper *C. fuscicollis* W
Pectoral Sandpiper *C. melanotus* AO
Sharp-tailed Sandpiper *C. acuminata* V
Dunlin *C. alpina* 78
Curlew Sandpiper *C. ferruginea* 78
Semi-palmated Sandpiper *C. pusilla* V
Western Sandpiper *C. mauri* V
Sanderling *C. alba* 78
Buff-breasted Sandpiper *Tryngites subruficollis* W
Broad-billed Sandpiper *Limicola falcinellus* W
Ruff *Philomachus pugnax* 80
Avocet *Recurvirostra avosetta* 80
Black-winged Stilt *Himantopus himantopus* W
Grey Phalarope *Phalaropus fulicarius* 80
Red-necked Phalarope *P. lobatus* 80
Wilson's Phalarope *P. tricolor* W
Stone Curlew *Burhinus oedicnemus* 80
Collared Pratincole *Glareola pratincola* W
Black-winged Pratincole *G. nordmanni* V
Cream-coloured Courser *Cursorius cursor* V
Great Skua *Stercorarius skua* 84
Pomarine Skua *S. pomarinus* AO
Arctic Skua *S. parasiticus* 84
Long-tailed Skua *S. longicaudus* AO
Ivory Gull *Pagophila eburnea* 80
Great Black-backed Gull *Larus marinus* 84
Lesser Black-backed Gull *L. fuscus* 84
Herring Gull *L. argentatus* 86
Ring-billed Gull *L. delawarensis* V
Common Gull *L. canus* 86
Glaucous Gull *L. hyperboreus* AO
Iceland Gull *L. glaucoides* AO
Slender-billed Gull *L. genei* V
Great Black-headed Gull *L. ichthyaetus* V
Mediterranean Gull *L. melanocephalus* AO
Laughing Gull *L. atricilla* V
Franklin's Gull *L. pipixcan* V
Bonaparte's Gull *L. philadelphia* W
Little Gull *L. minutus* AO
Black-headed Gull *L. ridibundus* 86
Sabine's Gull *L. sabinia* AO
Ross's Gull *Rhodostethia rosea* V
Kittiwake *Rissa tridactyla* 86
Black Tern *Chlidonias niger* 88
White-winged Black Tern *C. leucopterus* W
Whiskered Tern *C. hybrida* W
Gull-billed Tern *Gelochelidon nilotica* W
Caspian Tern *Hydroprogne caspia* W
Common Tern *Sterna hirundo* 88
Arctic Tern *S. paradisaea* 88
Roseate Tern *S. dougallii* 88
Sooty Tern *S. fuscata* V
Bridled Tern *S. anaethetus* V

Little Tern *S. albifrons* 88
Royal Tern *S. maxima* V
Sandwich Tern *S. sandvicensis* 88
Razorbill *Alca torda* 90
Little Auk *Plautus alle* AO
Guillemot *Uria aalge* 90
Brünnich's Guillemot *U. lomvia* V
Black Guillemot *Cepphus grylle* 90
Puffin *Fratercula arctica* 90
Pallas's Sandgrouse *Syrrhaptes paradoxus* V
Stock Dove *Columba oenas* 94
Rock Dove *C. livia* 94
Woodpigeon *C. palumbus* 94
Turtle Dove *Streptopelia turtur* 94
Rufous Turtle Dove *S. orientalis* V
Collared Dove *S. decaocto* 94
Cuckoo *Cuculus canorus* 94
Great Spotted Cuckoo *Clamator glandarius* V
Yellow-billed Cuckoo *Coccyzus americanus* W
Black-billed Cuckoo *C. erythropthalmus* V
Barn Owl *Tyto alba* 96
Scops Owl *Otus scops* W
Eagle Owl *Bubo bubo* V
Snowy Owl *Nyctea scandiaca* 96
Hawk Owl *Surnia ulula* V
Little Owl *Athene noctua* 96
Tawny Owl *Strix aluco* 96
Long-eared Owl *Asio otus* 96
Short-eared Owl *A. flammeus* 96
Tengmalm's Owl *Aegolius funereus* V
Nighthawk *Chordeiles minor* V
Nightjar *Caprimulgus europaeus* 98
Red-necked Nightjar *C. ruficollis* V
Egyptian Nightjar *C. aegyptius* V
Little Swift *Apus affinis* V
Swift *A. apus* 98
Alpine Swift *A. melba* W
Needle-tailed Swift *Hirundapus caudacutus* V
Kingfisher *Alcedo atthis* 98
Bee-eater *Merops apiaster* W
Blue-cheeked Bee-eater *M. superciliosus* V
Roller *Coracias garrulus* W
Hoopoe *Upupa epops* AO
Yellow-shafted Flicker *Colaptes auratus* E
Green Woodpecker *Picus viridis* 98
Great Spotted Woodpecker *Dendrocopos* ·
*major* 98
Lesser Spotted Woodpecker *D. minor* 98
Wryneck *Jynx torquilla* 98
Calandra Lark *Melanocorypha calandra* V
Bimaculated Lark *M. bimaculata* V
White-winged Lark *M. leucoptera* V
Short-toed Lark *Calandrella cinerea* W
Lesser Short-toed Lark *C. rufescens* V
Crested Lark *Galerida cristata* V
Woodlark *Lullula arborea* 100
Skylark *Alauda arvensis* 100
Shorelark *Eremophila alpestris* 100
Swallow *Hirundo rustica* 100
Red-rumped Swallow *H. daurica* V
House Martin *Delichon urbica* 100
Sand Martin *Riparia riparia* 100
Golden Oriole *Oriolus oriolus* AO
Raven *Corvus corax* 102
Carrion/Hooded Crow *C. corone* 102
Rook *C. frugilegus* 102

Jackdaw *C. monedula* 102
Magpie *Pica pica* 102
Nutcracker *Nucifraga caryocatactes* W
Jay *Garrulus glandarius* 102
Chough *Pyrrhocorax pyrrhocorax* 102
Great Tit *Parus major* 104
Blue Tit *P. caeruleus* 104
Coal Tit *P. ater* 104
Crested Tit *P. cristatus* 104
Marsh Tit *P. palustris* 104
Willow Tit *P. montanus* 104
Long-tailed Tit *Aegithalos caudatus* 106
Penduline Tit *Remiz pendulinus* V
Nuthatch *Sitta europaea* 106
Wallcreeper *Tichodroma muraria* V
Treecreeper *Certhia familiaris* 106
Wren *Troglodytes troglodytes* 106
Dipper *Cinclus cinclus* 106
Brown Thrasher *Toxostoma rufum* V
Bearded Reedling *Panurus biarmicus* 106
Mistle Thrush *Turdus viscivorus* 108
Fieldfare *T. pilaris* 108
Song Thrush *T. philomelos* 108
Redwing *T. iliacus* 108
Siberian Thrush *T. sibiricus* V
Eye-browed Thrush *T. obscurus* V
Dusky Thrush *T. naumanni* V
Black-throated Thrush *T. ruficollis* V
Ring Ouzel *T. torquatus* 108
Blackbird *T. merula* 108
American Robin *T. migratorius* V
White's Thrush *Zoothera dauma* W
Olive-backed Thrush *Hylocichla ustulata* V
Grey-cheeked Thrush *H. minima* V
Blue Rock Thrush *Monticola solitarius* E
Rock Thrush *M. saxatilis* V
Wheatear *Oenanthe oenanthe* 110
Desert Wheatear *O. deserti* V
Black-eared Wheatear *O. hispanica* W
Pied Wheatear *O. pleschanka* V
Isabelline Wheatear *O. isabellina* V
Black Wheatear *O. leucura* V
Stonechat *Saxicola torquatus* 110
Whinchat *S. rubetra* 110
Red-flanked Bluetail *Tarsiger cyanurus* V
Redstart *Phoenicurus phoenicurus* 110
Black Redstart *P. ochruros* 110
Nightingale *Luscinia megarhynchos* 110
Thrush Nightingale *L. luscinia* W
Bluethroat *L. svecica* AO
Robin *Erithacus rubecula* 110
Rufous Bush Robin *Cercotrichas galactotes* V
Cetti's Warbler *Cettia cetti* AO
Grasshopper Warbler *Locustella naevia* 112
Lanceolated Warbler *L. lanceolata* V
River Warbler *L. fluviatilis* V
Savi's Warbler *L. luscinioides* AO
Pallas' Grasshopper Warbler *L. certhiola* V
Moustached Warbler *Acrocephalus melanopogon* V
Thick-billed Warbler *A. aedon* V
Great Reed Warbler *A. arundinaceus* W
Reed Warbler *A. scirpaceus* 112
Marsh Warbler *A. palustris* AO
Blyth's Reed Warbler *A. dumetorum* V
Paddyfield Warbler *A. agricola* V

Sedge Warbler *A. schoenobaenus* 112
Aquatic Warbler *A. paludicola* AO
Melodius Warbler *Hippolais polyglotta* AO
Icterine Warbler *H. icterina* AO
Olivaceous Warbler *H. pallida* V
Booted Warbler *H. caligata* V
Blackcap *Sylvia atricapilla* 112
Barred Warbler *S. nisoria* AO
Orphean Warbler *S. hortensis* V
Garden Warbler *S. borin* 112
Whitethroat *S. communis* 114
Lesser Whitethroat *S. curruca* 114
Sardinian Warbler *S. melanocephala* V
Desert Warbler *S. nana* V
Subalpine Warbler *S. cantillans* W
Spectacled Warbler *S. conspicillata* V
Dartford Warbler *S. undata* 114
Fan-tailed Warbler *Cisticola juncidis* V
Willow Warbler *Phylloscopus trochilus* 114
Greenish Warbler *P. trochiloides* W
Chiffchaff *P. collybita* 114
Wood Warbler *P. sibilatrix* 114
Bonelli's Warbler *P. bonelli* W
Arctic Warbler *P. borealis* W
Yellow-browed Warbler *P. inornatus* AO
Pallas' Warbler *P. proregulus* W
Dusky Warbler *P. fuscatus* V
Radde's Warbler *P. schwarzi* V
Goldcrest *Regulus regulus* 116
Firecrest *R. ignicapillus* 116
Spotted Flycatcher *Muscicapa striata* 116
Pied Flycatcher *Ficedula hypoleuca* 116
Collared Flycatcher *F. albicollis* V
Red-breasted Flycatcher *F. parva* AO
Dunnock *Prunella modularis* 116
Alpine Accentor *P. collaris* V
Richard's Pipit *Anthus novaesseelandiae* AO
Tawny Pipit *A. campestris* AO
Meadow Pipit *A. pratensis* 118
Tree Pipit *A. trivialis* 118
Olive-backed Pipit *A. hodgsoni* V
Pechora Pipit *A. gustavi* V
Red-throated Pipit *A. cervinus* W
Rock/Water Pipit *A. spinoletta* 118
Pied/White Wagtail *Motacilla alba* 118
Grey Wagtail *M. cinerea* 118
Citrine Wagtail *M. citreola* V
Yellow/Blue-headed Wagtail *M. flava* 118
Waxwing *Bombycilla garrulus* 120
Great Grey Shrike *Lanius excubitor* AO
Lesser Grey Shrike *L. minor* W
Woodchat Shrike *L. senator* AO
Red-backed Shrike *L. collurio* 120
Starling *Sturnus vulgaris* 120
Rose-coloured Starling *S. roseus* AO
Red-eyed Vireo *Vireo olivaceus* V
Black-and-white Warbler *Mniotilta varia* V
Parula Warbler *Parula americana* V
Yellow Warbler *Dendroica petechia* V

Myrtle Warbler *D. coronata* V
Blackpoll Warbler *D. striata* V
Ovenbird *Seiurus aurocapillus* V
Northern Waterthrush *S. noveboracensis* V
Yellowthroat *Geothlypis trichas* V
Hooded Warbler *Wilsonia citrinia* V
American Redstart *Setophaga ruticilla* V
Bobolink *Dolichonyx oryzivorus* V
Baltimore Oriole *Icterus galbula* V
Evening Grosbeak *Hesperiphona vespertina* V
Blue Grosbeak *Guiraca caerulea* E
Hawfinch *Coccothraustes coccothraustes* 120
Greenfinch *Carduelis chloris* 120
Goldfinch *C. carduelis* 120
Siskin *C. spinus* 120
Linnet *Acanthis cannabina* 122
Twite *A. flavirostris* 122
Redpoll *A. flammea* 122
Arctic Redpoll *A. hornemanni* W
Citril Finch *Serinus citrinella* V
Serin *S. serinus* AO
Bullfinch *Pyrrhula pyrrhula* 122
Scarlet Rosefinch *Carpodacus erythrinus* AO
Pine Grosbeak *Pinicola enucleator* V
Crossbill *Loxia curvirostra* 122
Parrot Crossbill *L. pytyopsittacus* W
Two-barred Crossbill *L. leucoptera* W
Chaffinch *Fringilla coelebs* 122
Brambling *F. montifringilla* 122
Scarlet Tanager *Piranga olivacea* V
Summer Tanager *P. rubra* V
Corn Bunting *Emberiza calandra* 124
Yellowhammer *E. citrinella* 124
Pine Bunting *E. leucocephala* V
Red-headed Bunting *E. bruniceps* E
Black-headed Bunting *E. melanocephala* W
Yellow-breasted Bunting *E. aureola* W
Cirl Bunting *E. cirlus* 124
Cretzschmar's Bunting *E. caesia* V
Ortolan Bunting *E. hortulana* AO
Rock Bunting *E. cia* V
Rustic Bunting *E. rustica* W
Little Bunting *E. pusilla* W
Reed Bunting *E. schoeniclus* 124
Lapland Bunting *Calcarius lapponicus* AO
Snow Bunting *Plectrophenax nivalis* 124
Song Sparrow *Melospiza melodia* V
Fox Sparrow *Passerella ilaca* V
White-throated Sparrow *Zonotrichia albicollis* V
Slate-coloured Junco *Junco hyemalis* V
Rufous-sided Towhee *Pipilo erythrophthalmus* V
Rose-breasted Grosbeak *Pheuticus ludovicianus* V
House Sparrow *Passer domesticus* 124
Spanish Sparrow *P. hispaniolensis* V
Tree Sparrow *P. montanus* 124

# Divers family Gaviidae

**Black-throated Diver** *Gavia arctica* 56–68cm (22–27in) Like the other two divers, a large, almost wholly aquatic bird with a bulky body and stout neck. In summer with boldly patterned upperparts, grey head and back of neck, with the front of the neck and throat black edged by black and white streaks. In winter the upperparts are dark. Special note should be made of the bill which is more slender than that of the Great Northern, while the forehead is less steep. **Flight** Takes off with difficulty from water but once airborne flight is strong and rapid with the head held lower than the body, giving an unmistakable 'humped' appearance which is also typical of the other two species. White underparts contrast with dark upperparts; no wing-bar. **Voice** A guttural 'kwuk-kwuk-kwuk'. **Habitat** Lakes in summer; winters mainly on the coast though not infrequently inland on large lakes and reservoirs. **Distribution** Breeds locally in Scotland north from Argyll and Perth but not in Orkney or Shetland. Winters mainly off Scotland and the east and south-east coasts of England; rather rare elsewhere.

**Great Northern Diver** *Gavia immer* 68–81cm (27–32in) In summer has a black head with incomplete white neck bands and spotted underparts. In winter much like the Black-throated but generally larger size and much heavier bill are distinguishing features. **Flight** and **Voice** As for Black-throated. **Habitat** Lakes in summer; winters mainly on the coast, occasionally at inland waters. **Distribution** Mainly a winter visitor to Scotland, Ireland and south-west England. Birds occasionally summer in northern Scotland, a pair nesting in 1970.

**Red-throated Diver** *Gavia stellata* 53–58cm (21–23in) Our smallest diver; in summer has uniform dark grey upperparts, a grey head and sides of neck. The dull red throat patch may look black when viewed from a distance or in poor light. The back of the head and neck are streaked black and white. In winter looks whiter than the other divers and has a finely spotted back. At all seasons the up-tilted appearance of the rather slender bill is an important identification feature. **Flight** As for Black-throated. **Voice** A quacking 'kwuk-kwuk-kwuk'. **Habitat** Small pools to larger lakes on moorland; winters offshore though frequently visits inland waters. **Distribution** A few pairs breed in County Donegal, otherwise the highlands of Scotland including many islands are its stronghold. In winter may be found off all coasts, particularly in sheltered bays, harbours and larger estuaries.

winter

**Black-throated Diver**

summer

winter

summer

**Great Northern Diver**

winter

winter

**Red-throated Diver**

summer

# Grebes family Podicipitidae

**Great Crested Grebe** *Podiceps cristatus* 48cm (19in) Breeding adults have pronounced double-horned crests and reddish facial frills, the former reduced, the latter lost completely in winter. The thin red bill, very white cheeks and neck distinguish it from the slightly smaller Red-necked. **Flight** Conspicuous white wing-patches, while the long neck and trailing feet are typical of all grebes. **Voice** A barking 'gorr' and a crooning song. **Habitat** Large areas of open water required for breeding; in winter some move to sheltered coasts. **Distribution** Resident in many counties south from central Scotland; winters on all coasts.

**Red-necked Grebe** *Podiceps grisegena* 43cm (17in) Stockier built than Great Crested from which it may be distinguished in winter by the darker colour of the head extending below the eye, the sides of the neck dusky not white, and a black-tipped yellow bill. **Flight** Similar to Great Crested. **Voice** A high-pitched 'keck-keck'. **Habitat** In winter off coast; rare inland. **Distribution** Winter visitor, mainly to the east coast.

**Slavonian Grebe** *Podiceps auritus* 33cm (13in) Chestnut neck and underparts, black head with golden ear-tufts; bright colours lost in winter when it may be distinguished from Black-necked by its conspicuous white cheeks and straight bill. **Flight** Shows a white patch on trailing edge of wing. **Voice** A low rippling trill. **Habitat** Lakes and ponds in summer; mainly maritime in winter. **Distribution** Breeds on a few lakes in north-east Scotland; winters off all coasts.

**Black-necked Grebe** *Podiceps nigricollis* 30cm (12in) Black head and neck with downward pointing ear-tufts. The slightly up-tilted bill, steep forehead and black cheeks distinguish it in winter from Slavonian. **Flight** Longer wing-patch than Slavonian; wing-tips very dark. **Voice** A soft 'peeip'. **Habitat** Shallow lakes in summer; mainly on coast in winter. **Distribution** Breeds only at several sites in central Scotland; sporadic elsewhere; winters mainly on east and south coasts.

**Little Grebe** *Tachybaptus ruficollis* 27cm (10½in) Stockier built than the larger grebes. Dark brown with a chestnut throat and whitish yellow patch at the base of bill in summer; paler in winter. **Flight** No wing-patch. **Voice** A rippling trill. **Habitat** A wide variety of lowland waters; some move to harbours and estuaries in winter. **Distribution** Breeds in most areas.

**Great Crested Grebe**

winter

summer

**Great Crested Grebe**
summer

summer
**Red-necked Grebe**

winter

winter

winter

summer
**Slavonian Grebe**

summer

**Black-necked Grebe**

winter

summer

**Little Grebe**

**Manx Shearwater** *Puffinus puffinus* (family Procellariidae) 35cm (14in) Nocturnal at its colonies, spending the day in its nesting burrows or fishing out at sea. **Flight** A slender-bodied bird with long wings; at times tilting so that dark upperside then white underside is visible. Rapid flight; a few wing-beats followed by a period of gliding, often low over the waves. **Voice** Screaming, gurgling and crowing noises, chiefly heard at colonies. **Habitat** Pelagic, breeding on remote islands. **Distribution** Breeds on a small number of islands off western Great Britain and Ireland. Moves in winter to the east coast of Brazil.

**Gannet** *Sula bassana* (family Sulidae) 90cm (36in) Adults have gleaming white plumage with narrow black-tipped wings. The head and neck are yellowish buff. Immatures in their first year are dark blackish brown; adult plumage is attained in the fourth year. (The juvenile opposite is not to scale.) **Flight** Strong, the long wings and cigar-shaped body being distinctive. Feeds by plunge diving from heights up to 42 metres (140 feet). **Voice** A loud 'urrah-rah-rah-rah-rah', normally only heard at the colonies. **Habitat** Marine, rarely coming inland. Breeds mostly on small remote islands. **Distribution** Sixteen colonies in British Isles. Majority nests in Scotland. First year birds are migratory, moving to north-west African waters; most older birds in winter disperse generally through Britain and Biscayan waters.

**Cormorant** *Phalacrocorax carbo* (family Phalacrocoracidae) 90cm (36in) Slender-bodied bird having dark brown-black plumage with a white face-patch, and in the breeding season a white patch on the thighs. Immatures are pale brown above and white beneath. Swims rather low in the water and when at rest on land frequently adopts a drying posture with outspread wings. Dives from the surface with a distinct forward leap, in contrast to divers and grebes which disappear almost imperceptibly. **Flight** Fairly swift with rapid wing-beats. **Voice** A loud 'urrah', mainly at the nest. **Habitat** Offshore; also estuaries, harbours and frequently inland on rivers, lakes and reservoirs. **Distribution** Resident with colonies scattered along all coasts except between south-east Yorkshire and the Isle of Wight.

**Shag** *Phalacrocorax aristotelis* 76cm (30in) Dark glossy green, which looks black at a distance, with yellow at the base of the bill. Has a distinctive crest early in the breeding season. Immatures brown, only slightly paler beneath. **Flight** Similar to Cormorant but faster wing-beats. **Voice** A harsh croaking and various hissing noises at the nest. **Habitat** Off rocky coasts with rather few occurrences inland. **Distribution** Resident, breeding on all rocky coasts; usually as a scattering of pairs rather than large colonies, and with few between Northumberland and the Isle of Wight.

Manx Shearwater

juvenile

adult

Gannet

Cormorant

Shag

# Herons family Ardeidae

**Grey Heron** *Ardea cinerea* 90cm (36in) A grey back and wings. Underparts, head and neck white. Black band runs from the eye to end in a trailing crest. On the ground its long neck and legs are distinctive. Its prey—fish, small mammals, amphibians and reptiles—may be sought by wading through marshy ground, or by standing motionless in shallow water. **Flight** The neck is retracted while the legs trail; the large rounded wings, with outer parts black, are moved majestically giving an impression of tremendous power. **Voice** A harsh 'krarnk'. Croaking notes are delivered at nest. **Habitat** Found almost anywhere there is water of some form, be it mountain tarn or estuary. **Distribution** Resident breeding in trees throughout much of Great Britain and Ireland. Where there are no trees it will choose low sites amongst scrub or even nest on sea-cliff ledges. Britain's largest colony with 178 pairs is at RSPB reserve Northward Hill in Kent.

**Bittern** *Botaurus stellaris* 76cm (30in) A large golden brown bird with much darker mottles and bars. Very skulking in its habits. Normally adopts a rather hunched posture but when alarmed will stand erect with its bill pointed skywards. **Flight** Neck retracted, legs trailing in typical heron fashion. Broad brown wings move with a slow owl-like beat. **Voice** A harsh 'aarrk'; the much remarked upon booming is performed by the male only during the early spring and may be heard over great distances, depending on conditions. **Habitat** Requires large areas of dense reedbed with occasional pools of shallow open water. **Distribution** Formerly restricted to Norfolk and Suffolk, these counties still remaining the stronghold, but since the 1940s has bred in several others north to Lancashire and more recently to Wales. Breeds on RSPB reserves at Minsmere, Suffolk and Leighton Moss, Lancashire. In winter, particularly during hard weather, birds disperse widely from the breeding areas and may occur in quite small marshy patches.

**Spoonbill** *Platalea leucorodia* (family Threskiornithidae) 86cm (34in) White colouring and long broad bill, spoon shaped at the tip, are easy identification characters. Adults have a yellowish breast-band and in the breeding season head plumes; immatures lack these and have blackish wing-tips. **Flight** Neck outstretched in contrast to the herons; flies rather slowly with regular wing-beats. **Voice** Silent. **Habitat** Reedy areas, lagoons and estuaries. **Distribution** Non-breeding but regular visitor to East Anglia where it may occur in small parties; less frequent elsewhere.

Grey Heron

Grey Heron

Bittern

Bittern

Spoonbill

# Ducks, geese and swans family Anatidae

**Mallard** *Anas platyrhynchos* 58cm (25in) The largest, commonest and best known duck. Male readily recognizable by its green head and white ring around the neck. Female brown with distinctive blue speculum. During 'eclipse' or autumn moult the male looks similar to the female but has a yellow bill; female's is greenish and juvenile's reddish. **Flight** Rapid. The blue speculum bordered with white is found in both sexes. **Voice** Female a loud 'quack'; male a subdued 'queek'. **Habitat** Breeds close to inland waters of all sizes; moves to more open waters and to estuaries in winter. **Distribution** Resident in all areas.

**Gadwall** *Anas strepera* 51cm (20in) Male is dullest of dabbling ducks with grey plumage contrasting with black tail coverts. Female smaller than Mallard and with white underparts and black and white speculum. **Flight** Similar to Wigeon (page 44). **Voice** Female a soft 'quack'; male a deep nasal 'nheck'. **Habitat** Ponds and lakes with good cover. **Distribution** Breeds mainly in East Anglia; otherwise a winter visitor in small numbers to most parts.

**Pintail** *Anas acuta* 66cm (26in) A tall slender bird, males have an elongated tail and dark brown head. Females are pale brown with slender appearance, thin neck and pointed tail. **Flight** Fast. Male has green, white bordered speculum: female brown speculum. **Voice** Mainly silent. **Habitat** Chiefly fresh water in summer; larger lakes and estuaries in winter. **Distribution** A few breed in Scotland and eastern England; otherwise a winter visitor.

**Shoveler** *Anas clypeata* 51cm (20in) The enormous bill is the outstanding feature of both sexes. Both are heavier-looking than other dabbling ducks. Drake has green head, white breast and chestnut underparts. **Flight** Rather laboured, the wings having a setback appearance. Both sexes have blue forewings and green speculum. **Voice** Female similar to Mallard; male a gutteral 'took-took'. **Habitat** Shallow water with good cover. **Distribution** Breeds in small numbers throughout much of Great Britain and Ireland.

Mallard

♀

♂

Gadwall

♀

♂

Pintail

♀

♂

Shoveler

♀

♂

**Teal** *Anas crecca* 35cm (14in) Our smallest duck, males at a distance seeming to have a dark head in contrast to their grey body. Female similar to small Mallard. **Flight** Very agile, often in compact flocks. Both sexes have green speculum. They appear shorter necked than other species. **Voice** Female a high-pitched 'quack'; male a musical 'kritt'. **Habitat** Breeds amongst thick vegetation; winters on inland waters and estuaries. **Distribution** Resident; rather scattered in south; numerous in winter.

**Garganey** *Anas querquedula* 38cm (15in) More slender than Teal and in this country never in large flocks. The male's conspicuous eye-stripe distinguishes it from other species. **Voice** Female similar to Teal; male a low crackling. **Flight** Rapid and agile. Both sexes have blue-grey forewings and green specula. **Habitat** Shallow pools, ditches and creeks having plenty of cover. **Distribution** Summer visitor with less than 100 pairs breeding in south-east England; elsewhere a scarce passage visitor.

**Wigeon** *Anas penelope* 46cm (18in) Compact duck with a short bill. Male's buff cream and chestnut head and grey underparts distinctive. **Flight** Long narrow wings have a conspicuous white patch and green specula. **Voice** Female a purring note; males a distinctive whistling. **Habitat** Breeds close to inland waters; in winter largely estuarine and often seen grazing on fields. **Distribution** Breeds chiefly in northern Scotland; otherwise a numerous winter visitor, particularly large numbers on the RSPB's Ouse Washes reserve, Cambridgeshire.

**Scaup** *Aythya marila* 48cm (19in) Rather similar to Tufted Duck. Good identification characters are the grey back of the male and white facial mark of the female which is more pronounced than that of Tufted Duck. **Flight** In compact but irregular flocks or lines. Male distinguishable in good light from Tufted Duck by grey back. **Voice** Female a harsh 'karr-karr'; male generally silent. **Habitat** Breeds beside lochs and rivers; winters mainly on sheltered coasts. **Distribution** Occasionally breeds in Scotland; otherwise a winter visitor; up to 25,000 in the Forth.

**Tufted Duck** *Aythya fuligula* 43cm (17in) Only duck adorned with a tuft at back of head. **Flight** Rapid and like most diving duck has to patter along the water surface before taking off. **Voice** Female a growling 'kur-r-r-'; male in spring has a gentle whistle. **Habitat** Breeds on secluded lakes; winters on open fresh water. **Distribution** Breeds in eastern Britain; winters in all areas.

Teal

Garganey

Wigeon

Scaup

Tufted Duck

**Pochard** *Aythya ferina* 46cm (18in) The striking plumaged males are among the most easily identified diving ducks. The only duck with chestnut head, black breast and grey underparts. Female larger and paler than Tufted with no white facial markings. **Flight** Straight with rapid wing beats. **Voice** Generally silent; female in spring has a harsh 'kur-r-r'. **Habitat** Breeds in dense vegetation close to fresh water; occasionally coastal lagoons. **Distribution** Breeds mainly in south-east England; winters in all areas.

**Goldeneye** *Bucephala clangula* 46cm (18in) Has a distinctive head profile, the short bill and steep crown giving an almost triangular appearance. Neck distinctively white. **Flight** Wings produce a characteristic whistling sound. **Voice** Generally silent. **Habitat** Breeds in woodland close to water; winters mainly in estuaries and offshore. Seen on lochs in Scotland in spring and has bred in Inverness-shire woodland close to water. **Distribution** Winters in all areas.

**Common Scoter** *Melanitta nigra* 48cm (19in) The male, generally greatly outnumbering the browner female, is our only completely dark duck. **Flight** Strong, usually in lines low over the sea. **Voice** Female a harsh growl; male a variety of cooing notes. **Habitat** Breeds on lochs in hilly country; otherwise frequents the open sea close inshore. **Distribution** Small numbers breed in north-west Ireland and Scotland; non-breeders summer elsewhere; winters off all coasts.

**Long-tailed Duck** *Clangula hyemalis* 53cm (21in) Only duck combining a white body and dark wings and having an extremely short bill. Male has an extremely long tail. In winter it appears largely white, but in summer plumage it has a dark head and breast. **Flight** Usually low and swinging from side to side. **Voice** Female a soft 'quack'; male a musical 'ow-ow-ow'. **Habitat** Mainly maritime. **Distribution** Winter visitor mainly to east coast; smaller numbers in west.

Pochard

♀

♂

Goldeneye

♀

♂

Common Scoter

♀

♂

Long-tailed Duck

♀ winter

♂ winter

♂ summer

**Eider** *Somateria mollissima* 58cm (23in) Has a characteristic head profile, the bill continuing in a straight line from the forehead, and a thick set body. **Flight** Usually in single file just above the sea. **Voice** Female a grating 'kr-r-r'; male a moaning 'coo-roo-uh'. **Habitat** Maritime, rarely inland. **Distribution** Breeds in the northern counties of England and Ireland and throughout Scotland; non-breeders summer further south where wintering birds are also regularly encountered.

**Red-breasted Merganser** *Mergus serrator* 58cm (23in) Long slender profile and slender hooked bill separate it immediately from all other duck except larger Goosander. **Flight** Slender shape and large white wing-patches. **Voice** Female a harsh 'kar-r-r'; male usually silent. **Habitat** Breeds in vicinity of fresh water; frequents estuaries and seacoasts in winter. **Distribution** Breeds mainly in north-west Scotland and Ireland, but extending south in some western areas. Widespread elsewhere in winter.

**Goosander** *Mergus merganser* 66cm (26in) Larger than Mallard with a similar shape to Red-breasted Merganser, the head and neck patterns separating it from this species. **Flight** Usually low and showing a good deal of white. **Voice** As for Red-breasted Merganser. **Habitat** Lakes and rivers in wooded areas for breeding: mainly open fresh water in winter; not on coast in any numbers. **Distribution** Breeds throughout much of Scotland; has recently extended into northern England and Wales. Winters in many areas.

**Smew** *Mergus albellus* 41cm (16in) Shorter billed and more typically duck-shaped than other mergansers. White appearance of male should present no identification problems. Females—'redheads'—may possibly be confused with grebes but have a pure white throat and cheeks. **Flight** Takes wing very readily and has a rapid flight. **Voice** Silent. **Habitat** Lakes and reservoirs in winter. **Distribution** Winter visitor mainly to south-east England; rather scarce elsewhere and irregular in the west.

**Shelduck** *Tadorna tadorna* 61cm (24in) A large, strikingly marked duck, with an upright 'goose' posture. Females are a little duller than males and lack the knob at the base of the beak. **Flight** Slower wing-beats than other duck. **Voice** A loud 'ak-ak-ak-ak'. **Habitat** Estuaries, sandy and muddy coasts, though may travel several miles inland to breed. **Distribution** Breeds throughout Great Britain and Ireland in suitable areas. Is absent or occurs only in small numbers during late summer when the majority makes a moult migration to Germany, with some going to Bridgwater Bay, Somerset.

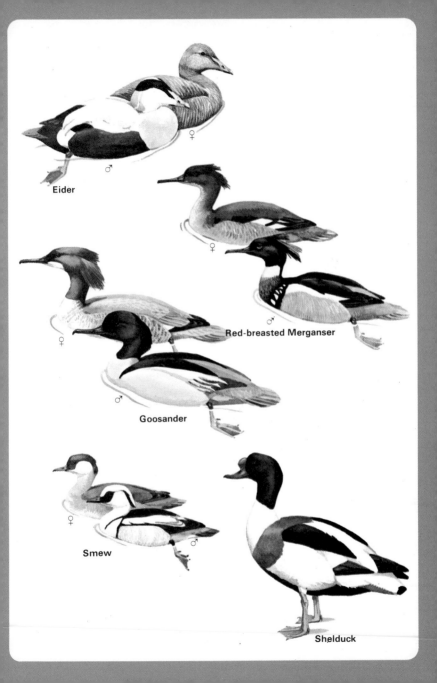

Eider

♀

♂

♀

Red-breasted Merganser

♂

♀

♂

Goosander

Smew

♀

♂

Shelduck

**Greylag Goose** *Anser anser* 76–89cm (30–35in) Largest of the grey geese having a heavy head and thick bill. Difficult to tell from other grey geese when viewed from a distance. **Flight** Pale grey forewing noticeable when a good view obtained. Often in flocks which adopt a 'V' formation. **Voice** Rather similar to the domestic goose, a loud 'aahung-ung-ung'. **Habitat** In breeding season, moorland areas with numerous small lochs. and in some cases small islands at sea. In winter, marshes and wet meadows from which it regularly flights to agricultural land. **Distribution** Breeds mainly in north-west Scotland where the outer Hebrides are its stronghold. Introduced birds have recently become established in several other parts of Britain. Main wintering area is in central Scotland.

**White-fronted Goose** *Anser albifrons* 66–76cm (26–30in) Darker coloured than Greylag and Pink-footed, adults having conspicuous black bars on the belly and a white patch at the base of the bill, though both features are absent in immatures. **Flight** Generally more active than other geese and although occurring in large flocks often disperses into family parties. **Voice** A laughing, rather high-pitched 'kow-kow'. **Habitat** Marshes, water meadows and saltings. **Distribution** The Greenland race winters mainly in Ireland and west Scotland, the European race in southern England and Wales.

**Bean Goose** *Anser fabalis* 71–89cm (28–35in) Browner and darker than other grey geese, with a somewhat long and slender build. Bill is longer and stouter than in Pink-footed. **Voice** Usually a gruff 'ung-unk', though not as noisy as most other geese. **Habitat** Marshes and wet meadows. **Distribution** Rather scarce winter visitor, occurring regularly only in south-west Scotland, Northumberland and East Anglia.

**Pink-footed Goose** *Anser brachyrhynchus* 61–76cm (24–30in) Rather like small Bean Goose, indeed some authorities consider them races of the same species. Main colour difference is the pale blue-grey upperparts contrasting with the dark head and neck. **Flight** The blue-grey forewings are conspicuous, though should not be confused with those of larger Greylag. **Voice** Perhaps the most noisy of all 'grey' geese, having a varied vocabulary including a musical 'wink-wink-wink'. **Habitat** Similar to Greylag, though is particularly fond of stubble and potato fields. **Distribution** Winter visitor, the first arriving in September, with particularly large concentrations in central Scotland, in Lincolnshire and East Anglia.

Greylag Goose

White-fronted Goose

Bean Goose

Pink-footed Goose

**Brent Goose** *Branta bernicla* 56–61 cm (22–24 in) Our smallest goose and, apart from the whitish neck patch, the only one to have its whole head and neck black. **Flight** Rather duck-like, usually in irregular flocks. **Voice** A croaking 'rronk'. **Habitat** Tidal flats and estuaries; rare inland. **Distribution** Winter visitor mainly on the east and south coast between Northumberland and Devon; scarce elsewhere.

**Barnacle Goose** *Branta leucopsis* 58–69 cm (23–27 in) Easily identified, even at a distance, by its contrasting black and white plumage. Has a particularly short bill. **Flight** Similar to other geese, though generally more reluctant to take off. **Voice** A barking 'ark' rapidly repeated. **Habitat** Pastures and marshes close to the shore. **Distribution** Winter visitor mainly to western Scotland and Ireland; scarce elsewhere but like other wildfowl some birds may be escapes or free-flying birds from collections.

**Canada Goose** *Branta canadensis* 92–102 cm (36–40 in) Much larger than the other two 'black' geese and has a mainly brown, not black and white, body. **Flight** Regularly flies in 'V' formation. **Voice** A trumpeting 'ker-honk'. **Habitat** Grassland close to freshwater lakes and pools. **Distribution** Breeds throughout much of England and parts of Wales; rather few in Scotland and Ireland. Mainly sedentary, though birds from Yorkshire visit the Moray Firth.

**Mute Swan** *Cygnus olor* 152 cm (60 in) Differs from the other two swans by having an orange bill with basal knob, while the carriage of the neck is less upright. **Flight** Heavy with 'sighing' sound produced by the wings. **Voice** Normally silent. **Habitat** A variety of inland waters, also sea lochs, estuaries and sheltered bays. **Distribution** Breeds throughout Great Britain and Ireland.

**Whooper Swan** *Cygnus cygnus* 152 cm (60 in) Usually holds neck stiffly erect. The bill, in contrast to that of Mute, is black with a large area of yellow at the base. **Flight** Wings create a swishing sound. **Voice** Our noisiest swan; has a bugle like 'ahng' in flight. **Habitat** Sheltered coasts, inland waters including the larger rivers. **Distribution** Small numbers summer in northern Scotland and has bred on several occasions; otherwise a winter visitor, mainly to Scotland and northern England.

**Bewick's Swan** *Cygnus bewickii* 122 cm (48 in) Resembles small Whooper, but the smaller area of yellow on the bill ends bluntly above the nostrils. **Flight** Similar to Whooper. **Voice** A rather goose-like gabble. **Habitat** Open waters and floodlands. **Distribution** Winter visitor mainly to England; scarce in Scotland.

Brent Goose

Barnacle Goose

Canada Goose

Bewick's Swan

Whooper Swan

Mute Swan

*Ducks and geese in flight. (All are to the same scale.)*

Mallard ♂

Gadwall ♂

Pintail ♂

Common Scoter ♂

Goldeneye ♂

Shoveler ♂

Pochard ♂

Goldeneye ♀

Long-tailed Duck ♂

Shoveler ♀

Wigeon ♂

Teal ♂

Garganey ♂

Scaup ♂

Tufted Duck ♂

Eider ♂

Red-breasted Merganser ♂

Goosander ♂

Smew ♀

Smew ♂

Red-breasted Merganser ♀

Goosander ♀

Shelduck

Greylag Goose

Bean Goose

Barnacle Goose

Pink-footed Goose

Brent Goose

# Eagles and their allies family Accipitridae

**Golden Eagle** *Aquila chrysaetos* 75–88cm (30–35in) Adults varying shades of brown, yellowish on the nape. Immatures have a white tail terminating in a black band, and white patches on the wings. **Flight** Powerful, gliding or soaring with occasional, leisurely wing-beats. When soaring, wings held horizontally in a shallow 'V'. Large size, projecting head, longer tail and uniform colouring distinguish it from Buzzard. **Habitat** Mountainous regions and remote coastal areas. **Distribution** Mainly in Scottish Highlands and western Isles; a few pairs in south-west Scotland and at least one pair in northern England where specially protected by RSPB wardening. Rare away from breeding areas.

**Buzzard** *Buteo buteo* 51–56cm (20–22in) Rather variable in plumage, particularly the amount of white on the underparts. **Flight** Often in soaring leisurely sweeps when the broad rounded wings, short head and broad, slightly rounded tail are characteristic. Often has a dark carpal mark. **Voice** A characteristic 'mewing' note. **Habitat** From barren hills and coastal districts to lower well-wooded areas. **Distribution** Breeds throughout much of Scotland, north-west England, Wales and the south-western counties of England east to Gloucestershire and Sussex. In Ireland breeds only in Ulster.

**Sparrowhawk** *Accipiter nisus* 28–38cm (11–15in) Adults have closely barred underparts; immatures are rather like the female but more boldly marked below. **Flight** Differs from falcons by having broad rounded wings. Normal flight a few wing-beats then a long glide. Hunts by flying fast, usually low amongst woodland or along hedgerows, dashing through openings or over bushes. Quite frequently soars and may rise to a considerable height. **Habitat** Usually in well-wooded cultivated country. **Distribution** Mainly in Scotland, western England, Wales and Ireland; has decreased and is now local in eastern England.

**Red Kite** *Milvus milvus* 61–63cm (24–25in) Plumage usually a good deal more rufous than Buzzard, especially tail, while the head is normally paler. **Flight** Long wings and long forked tail are easily seen when the bird soars overhead. A large whitish patch on the underside of the wings is distinctive. When gliding the wings are held level. **Habitat** Hilly country with well-wooded slopes. **Distribution** About twenty-six pairs currently breeding in central Wales, where extensively protected by RSPB, Nature Conservancy Council and others; rarely seen away from that area.

Golden Eagle

Buzzard

Sparrowhawk ♂

Red Kite

♀

**Marsh Harrier** *Circus aeruginosus* 48–56cm (19–22in) Largest of the harriers with a variable, mainly brown plumage, females, immature males and juveniles having creamy heads and shoulders. **Flight** The heaviest of the three harriers having broad rounded wings, while the adult male has extensive grey on the secondaries and grey tail. Hunts by quartering reedbeds and marshes, normally at no great height. **Habitat** Extensive reedbeds, swamps and marshes; occasionally to nearby cultivated areas. **Distribution** Mainly a rare summer visitor breeding only at a few sites in East Anglia where it may winter; occasionally elsewhere, but seen on passage in other areas. RSPB reserve at Minsmere, Suffolk, is its most regular breeding site (one or two pairs).

**Hen Harrier** *Circus cyaneus* 43–51cm (17–20in) More slender than Marsh, the sexes being easily distinguished. **Flight** Long, slender, slightly angled wings and long tail, the white rump patch being conspicuous in the female. Has a graceful buoyant action, a few wing-beats then a long shallow glide. **Habitat** Moorland and adjacent valleys including young conifer plantations; in winter moves to lowland heaths, rough pastures, marshes and dunes. **Distribution** Only bird of prey to have really increased its range in recent years. Now breeds in many areas in Scotland, parts of northern England, north Wales and throughout Ireland. In winter moves to other parts of Britain.

**Montagu's Harrier** *Circus pygargus* 41–46cm (16–18in) Male differs from male Hen by having a dark wing-bar and brown streaks on the belly. Female very similar to female Hen. **Flight** Slimmer wings and more buoyant flight than Hen. Separated from that species by an absence of the white rump in the male and a much smaller rump area in the female, though in the latter this feature is a variable and not clear-cut distinction. **Habitat** Marshes, rough commons, moorlands and large sand-dune areas. **Distribution** Summer visitor; now one of our rarest raptors with a handful of pairs breeding in south-west England and occasionally elsewhere.

**Osprey** *Pandion haliaetus* (family Pandionidae) 51–58cm (20–23in) Easily distinguished from other large birds of prey by means of its contrasting dark brown upperparts and snow white underparts. **Flight** Long, somewhat narrow, wings having a distinct angle at the carpal joint. When fishing flies at anything up to 30 metres (100 feet) above the water, hovering heavily before plunging after its prey. **Habitat** Lakes and rivers in wooded areas. **Distribution** Summer visitor with less than twenty pairs breeding in the Scottish Highlands after initial establishment at RSPB Loch Garten reserve; elsewhere on passage.

Marsh Harrier

Marsh Harrier

♀

♂

Hen Harrier

Hen Harrier

♀

♂

Montagu's Harrier

♂

Osprey

# Falcons family Falconidae

**Hobby** *Falco subbuteo* 30–36 cm (12–14 in) Longer winged and shorter tailed than Kestrel, with streaked underparts and rufous thighs. **Flight** Our most agile falcon; the long scythe-like wings and a short tail suggest a large Swift. Feeds on insects as much as birds, often continuing to catch the former until twilight. **Habitat** Downland and heaths with small woodlands; also well-timbered agricultural areas. **Distribution** Summer visitor; about 100 pairs breed in southern England, occasionally elsewhere; otherwise a casual visitor.

**Peregrine** *Falco peregrinus* 38–48 cm (15–19 in) Crow-sized, this is our largest breeding falcon. Dark-headed with conspicuous black moustachial stripes. **Flight** Rapid and often somewhat pigeon-like, with winnowing wings which are outspread during frequent lengthy glides. **Habitat** Mainly open country with cliffs or inland crags on which the birds nest; in winter many move to estuaries, marshes and not infrequently inland. **Distribution** Population much reduced during the late 1950s through effects of toxic chemical poisoning; has made some recovery but still not regained its former status. Breeds mainly in the Scottish Highlands, thence down the western side of Great Britain and in parts of Ireland; ranges further afield in winter.

**Merlin** *Falco columbarius* 27–33 cm (10½–13 in) Male is much smaller than other falcons and female a good deal browner than female Kestrel with which it might be confused. **Flight** Very dashing, usually low over the ground with frequent changes of direction, catching small birds after swift pursuits. Like the preceding falcons, the Merlin may hover briefly but not habitually like Kestrel. **Habitat** Hills and open moorland, coming to lower ground, saltings and dunes mainly in winter. **Distribution** Breeds mainly in Scotland, northern England and central Wales with a few in south-west England. Winters in all coastal areas.

**Kestrel** *Falco tinnunculus* 33–36 cm (13–14 in) Males should not be confused with any other bird of prey, while the longer pointed wings distinguish the female from Sparrowhawk. **Flight** Generally slower than other falcons though with rapid wing-beats; the frequent and lengthy hovering is distinctive. **Habitat** Almost ubiquitous from city centres to open country and the coast. **Distribution** Breeds throughout Great Britain and Ireland.

Hobby

Peregrine juvenile

Peregrine ♂

Merlin ♂ ♀

Kestrel ♀ ♂

*Birds of prey and owls in flight. (Birds with the same accompanying symbol are to the same scale. Those without a symbol are not to scale.)*

**Sparrowhawk** ○
♂

**Red Kite** ○

**Buzzard** ○

**Sparrowhawk** ○
♀

**Marsh Harrier**
♂

**Hen Harrier**
♂

**Montagu's Harrier**
♂

**Marsh Harrier**
♀ juvenile

**Hen Harrier**
♀ juvenile

**Montagu's Harrier**
♀ juvenile

Peregrine ○
♀

Osprey

Osprey ○

Osprey

Golden
Eagle

Long-eared
Owl ○

Short-eared
Owl ○

Short-eared
Owl

Kestrel

Merlin

Golden Eagle
sub-adult

Kestrel ○

Merlin ○

# Grouse family Tetraonidae

**Red Grouse** *Lagopus lagopus* 32–41 cm (13–16 in) A rather stout bird easily recognizable with its dark red-brown plumage. Possibly confused only with the female Black, though is smaller, redder coloured and has a rounded unforked tail. **Flight** Flies with rapid beats of its short wings interspersed with long glides low over the ground. **Voice** A cackling 'kowk, kok-ok-ok-ok', while the male in display is the source of the well-known moorland sound 'go-bak, bak-bak-bak'. **Habitat** Upland moors where heather is well established. **Distribution** Breeds throughout Scotland and much of northern England and Ireland, parts of Wales, Devon and Cornwall.

**Ptarmigan** *Lagopus mutus* 32–36 cm (13–14 in) Its white wings distinguish it at all seasons and no other gamebird is completely white in winter. Like other grouse, the Ptarmigan has feathered legs. **Flight** Similar to Red Grouse; often flushed only at the last moment; on landing merges immediately with its surroundings. **Voice** Mainly a harsh croak. **Habitat** Barren areas on or close to mountain tops; even during severe weather moves only to slightly lower ground. **Distribution** Scotland, mainly on mountains over 900 metres (3,000 feet) but lower in some areas, especially in north-west.

**Black Grouse** *Lyrurus tetrix* male 53 cm (21 in); female 41 cm (16 in) The male can hardly be confused with any other species. Females are browner than Red, while they are smaller and less boldly marked than female Capercaillie. **Flight** Rapid wing-beats; low when amongst cover but rises over open country. **Voice** A sneezing 'tch-sheew', while the male during display has various bubbling notes and females a loud 'chuck-chuk'. **Habitat** Moorland fringes and sparsely wooded heaths, often amongst developing conifer plantations. **Distribution** Scotland, though not extreme north, northern England, parts of Wales, Exmoor and the Quantocks.

**Capercaillie** *Tetrao urogallus* male 86 cm (34 in); female 62 cm (24 in) Turkey-sized male is unmistakable; females might be confused with female Black Grouse but are larger, have a rufous breast patch and a rounded tail. **Flight** Noisy when breaking cover. Often perches in trees. **Voice** Males mainly silent except during display; females a harsh 'kok-kok'. **Habitat** Mainly mature coniferous woodland but regularly moves to mixed areas in winter. **Distribution** Sedentary, breeding in the eastern Highlands; attempted introduction in north-west England.

Red Grouse

Ptarmigan
♂ winter
♀ autumn

Black Grouse
♂
♀

Capercaillie
♀
♂

# Partridges, pheasants family Phasianidae

**Red-legged Partridge** *Alectoris rufa* 34cm (13½in) Larger than Grey from which it may be distinguished by its white cheeks, throat bordered with black and by its heavily barred flanks. Juveniles are not so prominently marked and are then not unlike juvenile Grey, though have spots rather than streaks. **Flight** Usually prefers to run at the approach of danger, but will fly swiftly when flushed, the flocks — 'coveys' — usually dispersing. **Voice** A harsh 'chuka-chuka'. **Habitat** Fields, heaths and downs. **Distribution** An introduced resident, breeding mainly in central and southern England; also frequently introduced, though with variable success, elsewhere.

**Grey Partridge** *Perdix perdix* 30cm (12in) Main identification points are the pale chestnut head and grey neck, while males have a conspicuous dark mark on the lower breast. **Flight** Short rounded wings and a rufous tail; usually flies low over the ground. **Voice** A loud grating 'kar-wic'. **Habitat** Chiefly on arable land, but also occurs on heaths, sand-dunes, moorlands and marshes. **Distribution** Breeds throughout most of Great Britain and Ireland; less numerous in the north and west, numbers declining in recent years.

**Quail** *Coturnix coturnix* 18cm (7in) Rather like a miniature Grey Partridge though of slighter build and a more sandy colour. Sexes rather similar though the female lacks the black throat markings of the male. **Flight** Most reluctant to be flushed, and then only travels for a short distance low over the ground. Much prefers to hide or run from danger. **Voice** The characteristic 'quic-ic-ic', often interpreted as 'wet-my-lips', may be heard during the spring and early summer, often at some distance from the bird and not infrequently at night. Quite often calling birds provide the only indication that this species is present. **Habitat** Rough grasslands and cereal crops. **Distribution** Summer visitor in variable though rarely large numbers to Great Britain and Ireland. Has nested, though rarely annually in many counties, most frequently in southern England, though may do so north to Shetland.

**Pheasant** *Phasianus colchicus* male 66–89cm (30–35in); female 53–63cm (21–25in) The male is unmistakable with its bright colours and long tail. The browner female has a shorter tail though only immatures may possibly be confused with a partridge. **Flight** Prefers to run for cover; otherwise a noisy take-off, rapid wing-beats and, before landing, a long glide. **Voice** A strident 'karrk-karrk'. **Habitat** Woods and areas of thick cover. **Distribution** Resident, breeding throughout most of Great Britain and Ireland.

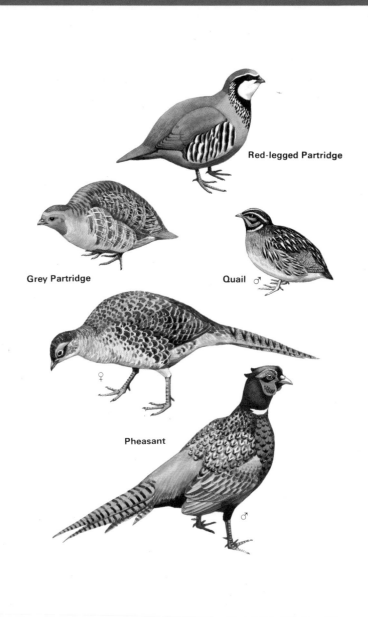

Red-legged Partridge

Grey Partridge

Quail ♂

Pheasant ♀

Pheasant ♂

# Crakes, rails, Coot family Rallidae

**Water Rail** *Rallus aquaticus* 28cm (11in) A secretive species but when visible the long red bill is an excellent identification feature. Whitish undertail coverts, not so conspicuous as in Moorhen. Olive brown upperparts and black and white flanks. **Flight** Weak and fluttering with dangling legs and usually of only short duration. **Voice** A variety of groans, grunts and squeaks, together with a persistent 'gep-gep' call. Often heard after dark. **Habitat** Reedbeds, swampy margins of ponds, rivers and overgrown ditches. **Distribution** Main breeding areas are in East Anglia and in Ireland; more scattered in other areas but is probably overlooked. More widespread in winter when immigration takes place.

**Corncrake** *Crex crex* 27cm (10½in) Rather like a small slender gamebird, though rarely seen until flushed. Yellowish buff and well-marked upperparts. **Flight** Will run away when disturbed but when flushed its chestnut wings, dangling legs and sluggish flight distinguish it from partridges and Quail. **Voice** A rasping continuous 'crek-crek' which may be heard at night as much as during the day. Can be imitated by striking a piece of wood across a comb which may on occasions attract a bird close to the observer. **Habitat** Mainly lush grasslands. **Distribution** Summer visitor, now only breeding regularly in parts of northern England, western Scotland and Ireland; sporadic elsewhere, though regularly encountered on passage when calling birds may remain for some days.

**Moorhen** *Gallinula chloropus* 33cm (13in) One of our best known waterside birds. Adults and young continually flirt tail to show conspicuous white undertail coverts. **Flight** Rather laboured with legs either dangling or projecting behind the tail; usually prefers to run for cover. **Voice** A loud 'kr-r-rk' or 'kittac'. **Habitat** All waterside areas with cover. **Distribution** Breeds widely throughout Great Britain and Ireland.

**Coot** *Fulica atra* 38cm (15in) Stoutly built with a white frontal shield and bill. Often in large flocks and generally very quarrelsome. **Flight** Patters along the surface before taking off, feet outstretched once airborne. **Voice** A high pitched 'kowk'. **Habitat** Requires larger, more open waters than Moorhen, and in winter may visit estuaries and sheltered bays during hard weather. **Distribution** Resident breeding throughout much of Great Britain and Ireland, numbers being augmented in winter by continental immigrants.

**Water Rail**

**Corncrake**

**Moorhen**

**Coot**

# Waders

**Oystercatcher** *Haematopus ostralegus* (family Haematopodidae) 43cm (17in) One of our most conspicuous and easily recognizable waders. having pied plumage, an orange-red bill and red legs. **Flight** Flies with shallow wing-beats. **Voice** A noisy 'kleep-kleep'. **Habitat** Found mainly along coast and on estuaries; extends to lakes, rivers and moorland in northern districts. **Distribution** Resident, breeding on virtually all coasts and inland from the Pennines northwards.

**Lapwing** *Vanellus vanellus* (family Charadriidae) 30cm (12in) our only wader to support a crest which, when viewed at close quarters, can be clearly seen as metallic green as are the upperparts. **Flight** Broad, rounded wings and leisurely, often erratic, flight. **Voice** A wheezy 'kee-wi'. **Habitat** Breeds mainly on agricultural areas; many move in winter to estuary regions. **Distribution** Breeds throughout Great Britain and Ireland with a considerable winter immigration.

**Ringed Plover** *Charadrius hiaticula* 19cm ($7\frac{1}{2}$in) One of the smaller waders, robustly built and with a short bill. Usually very active. **Flight** Rapid and low. **Voice** A liquid 'too-li'. **Habitat** Breeds mainly along the shore where it is currently decreasing due to disturbance; also inland in the north. **Distribution** Breeds on all coasts apart from the south-west of England; inland in parts of Scotland, Ireland and East Anglia. More numerous in winter.

**Little Ringed Plover** *Charadrius dubius* 15cm (6in) Difficult to tell from Ringed Plover though has a white line on the forehead, flesh-coloured legs, no wing-bar in flight. **Voice** 'Pee-u'. **Habitat** Gravel pits, rivers and lakes. **Distribution** Summer visitor, extending its range through south and central England.

**Grey Plover** *Pluvialis squatarola* 28cm (11in) Though migrants may be in breeding plumage, mainly seen in winter plumage when uniform grey colour distinguishes it from Golden Plover. **Flight** Conspicuous black axillaries. **Voice** High-pitched 'tlee-oo-ee'. **Habitat** Estuaries. **Distribution** Passage migrant and winter visitor.

**Golden Plover** *Pluvialis apricaria* 28cm (11in) Has distinctive black and gold spangled upperparts; browner in winter when throat and underparts lack black markings. **Flight** Rapid, often in compact flocks. **Voice** A liquid 'tlui'. **Habitat** Breeds on moorland, moving to lower agricultural land in winter. Regular on coast in some areas. **Distribution** Breeds mainly from the southern Pennines northwards; rather few in Wales and Ireland, but winters in all districts.

Oystercatcher

Lapwing

Little Ringed Plover

Ringed Plover

summer

winter

Grey Plover

summer

winter

Golden Plover

**Dotterel** *Eudromias morinellus* 22cm (8½in) A rather striking wader in summer plumage; greyish brown on autumn passage though retaining the prominent eye-stripes and pectoral band. Often very tame. **Flight** Similar to Golden Plover. **Voice** A trilling 'wit-e-wee'. **Habitat** Breeds on barren mountains above 780 metres (2,500 feet). Passage birds occur on pastures, heaths and marshes while in the Netherlands it breeds on arable land. **Distribution** Summer visitor in small numbers breeding in the central Highlands; occasionally elsewhere.

**Turnstone** *Arenaria interpres* 23cm (9in) Basically a black and white stocky, short-billed wader; upperparts considerably brighter in summer but even then inconspicuous among rocks, pebbles and seaweed. **Flight** Takes flight reluctantly and usually flies for only a short distance somewhat slowly. **Voice** A twittering 'kititit'. **Habitat** Rocky or pebble shores; in sandy estuaries only where weed-covered reefs occur. **Distribution** Mainly a winter visitor to all coasts though non-breeders summer in many areas.

**Snipe** *Gallinago gallinago* (family Scolopacidae) 27cm (10½in) The brown plumage and secretive habits of this species mean that it is rarely seen until flushed from cover. **Flight** When flushed zig-zags away and often 'towers' the long bill often being easily visible. **Voice** Spring note a persistent 'chick-ka', while during display flights the well-known 'drumming' may be heard. This is made as the bird dives about the sky, the outer tail feathers producing short bursts of vibrations. When flushed the birds repeatedly make a harsh 'krepe'. **Habitat** Boggy areas with good cover. **Distribution** Resident breeding throughout much of Great Britain and Ireland.

**Jack Snipe** *Lymnocryptes minimus* 19cm (7½in) Like a miniature Snipe, but has a relatively shorter bill. Difficult to observe. **Flight** Rises from ground at last minute and instead of towering usually drops again within a few yards. **Voice** Normally silent except for an occasional weak 'skaap'. **Habitat** Marshy areas. **Distribution** Winter visitor, usually in small numbers to all areas.

**Woodcock** *Scolopax rusticola* 34cm (13½in) Like a big, stocky Snipe, usually flushed in woodland. Has mainly crepuscular habits. **Flight** Rises noisily and dodges rapidly away. The 'roding' display is a circuit of slow, rather owl-like wingbeats, usually just above the trees. **Voice** Males when 'roding' have a characteristic 'si-wick' note and a quiet double grunting note; otherwise mainly silent. **Habitat** Damp woodlands. **Distribution** Breeds throughout much of Great Britain and Ireland with immigration taking place each autumn from the Continent, so that in some areas it may be locally abundant.

summer

winter

summer

**Dotterel**

**Turnstone**

**Snipe**

**Jack Snipe**

**Woodcock**

**Curlew** *Numenius arquata* 48–64cm (19–25in) The largest wader with long legs, a long down-curved bill and buffish brown streaked plumage. **Flight** Takes off at the slightest hint of danger or disturbance and flies strongly with regular, rather gull-like wing-beats. **Voice** Varied, but the loud 'coorwee coorwee' notes are familiar in many areas. Also has a series of liquid bubbling notes heard mainly in spring. **Habitat** Breeds mainly in upland areas though does occur at lower altitudes when it chooses wet meadows, heaths and even dunes. Winters mainly on estuaries but also inland on wet meadows. **Distribution** Breeds throughout much of Great Britain and Ireland except for south-east England; common visitor to all estuary areas in winter.

**Whimbrel** *Numenius phaeopus* 38–41cm (15–16in) Like rather small Curlew with relatively shorter bill. When seen at fairly close range its head pattern is distinctive. **Flight** More rapid wing-beats than Curlew. **Voice** The best distinguishing feature from its larger relative, the main call being a tittering 'titti-titti-titti'; also has a bubbling Curlew-like song. **Habitat** Breeds on moorlands; passage birds occur mainly on estuaries, sometimes on rocky shores. **Distribution** Summer visitor, breeding in Orkney and Shetland with a few pairs in the north Highlands; elsewhere occurs on passage with a few overwintering.

**Black-tailed Godwit** *Limosa limosa* 38–43cm (15–17in) A tall, slender wading bird with long legs and a long straight bill. In summer the head, neck and breast are bright chestnut, with blackish markings on both upper and underparts. **Flight** Feet project noticeably beyond tail while the broad white wing-bar and bold tail pattern distinguish it from the other large waders, with which it might be confused. **Voice** A loud 'wicka-wicka' heard in flight. **Habitat** In breeding season mainly rough damp pastures, water meadows and the like. Estuaries and nearby areas in winter, but also visits freshwater marshes, sewage farms and reservoir margins. **Distribution** One regular breeding site in Cambridgeshire, especially at RSPB Ouse Washes reserve; sporadic elsewhere. Frequent on passage elsewhere with many wintering, particularly in the south.

**Bar-tailed Godwit** *Limosa lapponica* 35–38cm (14–15in) Very similar to Black-tailed, but shorter legs, slightly upturned bill and in summer the whole of the underparts chestnut-red. In winter plumage not unlike that of Curlew. **Flight** Feet project only slightly beyond tail; rump whitish and no wing-bar. **Voice** 'Kirruc-kirruc'. **Habitat** Sandy shores and estuaries; rare inland. **Distribution** Mainly a passage and winter visitor to all coasts; a few summer.

Curlew

Whimbrel

winter

Bar-tailed Godwit

summer

winter

Black-tailed Godwit

**Green Sandpiper** *Tringa ochropus* 23cm (9in) A shy bird with dark upperparts, conspicuous white rump and greenish legs. **Flight** When flushed looks not unlike large House Martin and usually adopts a towering erratic flight with jerky, rather Snipe-like wing-beats. **Voice** A ringing 'weet-a-weet'. **Habitat** Occurs beside lakes, ponds, ditches and estuary gutters, usually where there is shelter. **Distribution** Mainly a passage migrant to England, Wales and eastern Scotland; rather few elsewhere. A few overwinter.

**Wood Sandpiper** *Tringa glareola* 20cm (8in) Plumage at rest and in flight does not have the contrast of Green Sandpiper, being paler above. **Flight** Shows white rump and feet project beyond tail, but does not look so 'black-and-white' as Green Sandpiper. **Voice** An excited 'chiff-iff'. **Habitat** Breeds in swampy woodlands; on passage visits small pools, creeks, sewage farms and lake margins. **Distribution** A few pairs now breed in north-east Scotland; otherwise seen on passage, mainly in south-east.

**Common Sandpiper** *Tringa hypoleucos* 20cm (7¾in) A small slender wader with a rather horizontal stance and continual bobbing action. **Flight** Usually low with rapid but shallow wing-beats and frequent glides. **Voice** When flushed a piping 'twee-ee-ee'. **Habitat** Breeds close to the gravel banks of lakes and rivers, chiefly in upland districts. On passage occurs widely inland and often at coast. **Distribution** Breeds mainly in northern and western Britain, though no further south than mid-Wales. Passage birds encountered almost anywhere, with a few over-wintering.

**Redshank** *Tringa totanus* 28cm (11in) A brown wader with a medium length bill and striking orange-red legs. **Flight** White hind edge of wings and white rump conspicuous. **Voice** Noisy; alarm call a loud 'tew-hee-hee'. **Habitat** Breeds on grassy meadows, coastal saltings and low moorlands; otherwise very much an estuarine species. **Distribution** Resident, breeding in most counties.

**Spotted Redshank** *Tringa erythropus* 30cm (12in) In summer its mainly black plumage is unmistakable. In winter, a pale bird, more slender than Redshank; white rump but no wing markings. **Flight** Strong though erratic, with projecting legs. **Voice** A clear 'tchu-it'. **Habitat** Coastal areas and inland pools. **Distribution** Mainly an autumn passage migrant, though some seen midsummer while others overwinter.

**Greenshank** *Tringa nebularia* 30cm (12in) A tall grey-white wader with a long, slightly upturned bill. **Flight** No wing markings, conspicuous white rump extending up the lower back. **Voice** A loud 'tew-ew-tew'. **Habitat** Breeds on moorland with pools; winters on estuaries. **Distribution** Breeds in the north-west Highlands; elsewhere a passage migrant and winter visitor.

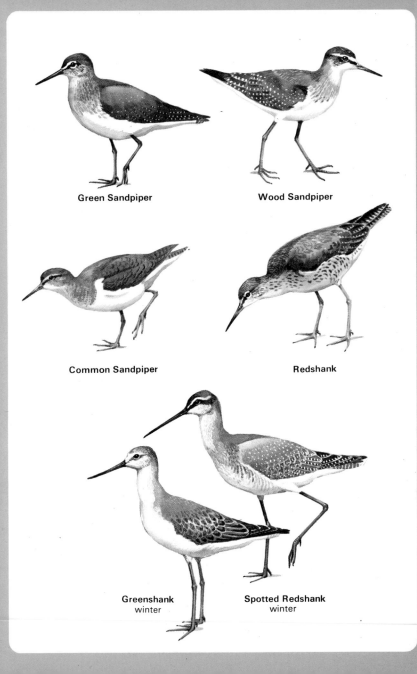

Green Sandpiper

Wood Sandpiper

Common Sandpiper

Redshank

Greenshank
winter

Spotted Redshank
winter

**Knot** *Calidris canutus* 25cm (10in) A greyish, short-billed wader midway in size between Redshank and Dunlin; of stocky build with a short neck. May show reddish underparts in spring and autumn. **Flight** Often in large compact flocks. Has a rather indistinct pale wing-bar and a pale rump and tail. **Voice** In flight a mellow 'twit-wit'. **Habitat** Mainly estuaries. **Distribution** Passage migrant and winter visitor, occasional in summer.

**Purple Sandpiper** *Calidris maritima* 21cm (8$\frac{1}{4}$in) Slightly larger and darker than Dunlin, its short yellow legs providing a rather portly appearance. **Flight** Swift, direct and usually of short duration. **Voice** Generally silent, though when flushed has a piping 'wee-it'. **Habitat** Rocky shores, weed covered piers and groynes. **Distribution** Passage migrant and winter visitor to rocky coasts.

**Little Stint** *Calidris minuta* 13cm (5$\frac{1}{4}$in) One of our smallest waders; rather like miniature Dunlin but with short, straight bill. **Flight** Rapid, its narrow wing-bar not conspicuous. **Voice** A sharp 'chik'. **Habitat** Estuaries and not infrequently inland at reservoirs, sewage farms and lakes. **Distribution** Passage migrant, mainly in autumn, chiefly on the east coast.

**Dunlin** *Calidris alpina* 16–19cm (6$\frac{3}{4}$–7$\frac{1}{2}$in) Our commonest and most numerous small wader with a long, slightly down-curved bill. The black belly patch is conspicuous in summer. **Flight** Usually in flocks which wheel and twist, the birds in complete unison, first with white undersides showing, then darker upperparts. **Voice** A weak 'treap'. **Habitat** Breeds on moorland with pools and boggy areas; mainly on estuaries in winter but small numbers at inland waters. **Distribution** Breeds in Scotland and northern England, sparingly in Wales and Ireland; elsewhere a numerous passage and winter visitor.

**Curlew Sandpiper** *Calidris ferruginea* 19cm (7$\frac{1}{2}$in) In winter plumage looks like slender Dunlin, but has a paler breast, brighter eye-stripe and a more slender down-curved bill. **Flight** Similar to Dunlin and has the same wing-bar, but unlike that species the rump is distinctly white. **Voice** A soft 'chirrip'. **Habitat** Estuaries and sometimes inland. **Distribution** Mainly a passage migrant; more numerous in autumn and chiefly on the east coast.

**Sanderling** *Calidris alba* 20cm (8in) A very active bird, almost ceaseless in its movements. Virtually white in winter plumage. Bill stouter and shorter than in Dunlin. **Flight** Reluctant to take off but when it does so shows a bright white wing-bar. **Voice** A liquid 'quit quit'. **Habitat** Sandy shores. **Distribution** Passage migrant but also winters on most coasts.

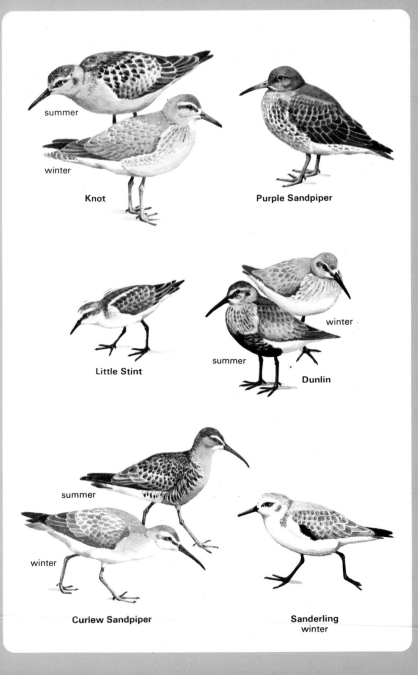

summer

winter

**Knot**

**Purple Sandpiper**

**Little Stint**

winter

summer

**Dunlin**

summer

winter

**Curlew Sandpiper**

**Sanderling**
winter

**Ruff** *Philomachus pugnax* male 28–30cm (11–12in); female 22–25cm (8½–10in) Only males in summer show the full breeding plumage; otherwise both sexes and immatures look rather nondescript and vary considerably in size and colour of legs. **Flight** Somewhat like that of Redshank. The oval white patch on each side of the otherwise dark tail is a good feature. **Voice** A low 'tu-whit'. **Habitat** Ouse Washes, water meadows, including RSPB reserve, are only known breeding grounds. On passage visits the shores of lakes, gravel pits and sewage farms, rather infrequent on estuaries. **Distribution** Breeds at one site in Cambridgeshire; otherwise a passage or winter visitor, most numerous in eastern districts.

**Avocet** *Recurvirostra avosetta* (family Recurvirostridae) 43cm (17in) One of our most unmistakable birds with a long, 9·3cm (3¾in), upturned bill. **Flight** Black and white pattern conspicuous as are the long bill and feet projecting well beyond the tail. **Voice** Noisy, particularly at the nest; main call a clear 'klooit'. **Habitat** Breeds beside shallow brackish lagoons; winters on estuaries. **Distribution** Summer visitor, almost all breeding at RSPB reserves at Havergate and Minsmere, Suffolk. Some birds regularly winter in south-west England; otherwise only seen on passage, rather rarely in most districts.

**Grey Phalarope** *Phalaropus fulicarius* (family Phalaropodidae) 20·5cm (8in) Phalaropes are the only waders which regularly swim which they do buoyantly, looking like miniature gulls. May often be seen spinning on the surface, eating invertebrates brought up by this action. **Flight** Most reluctant to take off and over short distances rather weak and erratic. **Voice** A soft 'twit'. **Habitat** Mainly at sea; occasionally on inland waters. **Distribution** Passage migrant, chiefly in autumn.

**Red-necked Phalarope** *Phalaropus lobatus* 17cm (6½in) In summer the female is much brighter coloured than the male. Distinguished in winter from Grey by its smaller size, more slender bill and darker back with white markings. **Flight** Similar to Grey. **Voice** A low-pitched 'whit'. **Habitat** Breeds on marshy ground near open water. **Distribution** Summer visitor, breeding in small numbers in north and north-west Scotland with a single colony in Ireland. Elsewhere a scarce passage migrant.

**Stone Curlew** *Burhinus oedicnemus* (family Burhinidae) 41cm (16in) A large round-headed bird having streaked sandy plumage, yellow eyes and legs. **Flight** Rather slow wing-beats with trailing legs; two whitish wing-bars. **Voice** Shrill and Curlew-like. **Habitat** Sandy heaths, waste land and chalk uplands. **Distribution** Summer visitor, breeding sparsely in several south-eastern counties; rarely seen elsewhere.

Ruff ♀

Ruff summer ♂

Grey Phalarope winter

Avocet

Stone Curlew

summer ♀

winter

Red-necked Phalarope

Waders in flight. (Birds with the same accompanying symbol are to the same scale. Those without a symbol are not to scale.)

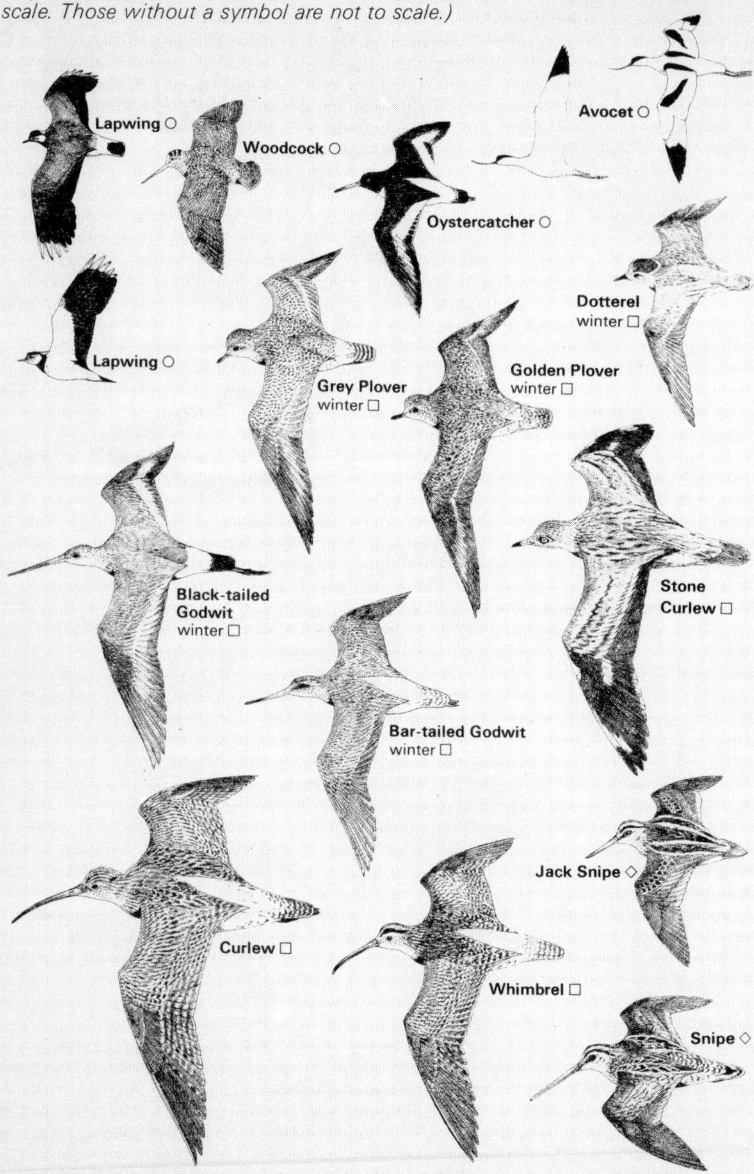

Lapwing ○

Woodcock ○

Avocet ○

Oystercatcher ○

Lapwing ○

Grey Plover winter □

Dotterel winter □

Golden Plover winter □

Black-tailed Godwit winter □

Stone Curlew □

Bar-tailed Godwit winter □

Curlew □

Jack Snipe ◇

Whimbrel □

Snipe ◇

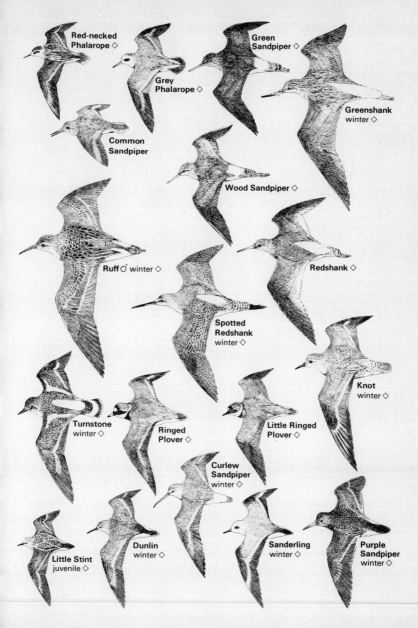

Red-necked Phalarope ◇

Grey Phalarope ◇

Green Sandpiper ◇

Greenshank winter ◇

Common Sandpiper

Wood Sandpiper ◇

Ruff ♂ winter ◇

Redshank ◇

Spotted Redshank winter ◇

Knot winter ◇

Turnstone winter ◇

Ringed Plover ◇

Little Ringed Plover ◇

Curlew Sandpiper winter ◇

Little Stint juvenile ◇

Dunlin winter ◇

Sanderling winter ◇

Purple Sandpiper winter ◇

# Skuas family Stercorariidae

**Great Skua** *Stercorarius skua* 58cm (23in) Much stockier built than rather similar sized Herring Gull, and much darker plumaged than immatures of that species. **Flight** Heavier than a gull but surprisingly swift when pursuing other birds or at the breeding grounds. Large and conspicuous white wing-patches. **Voice** A loud 'hah-hah-hah-hah' heard at the breeding colonies. **Habitat** Maritime except in breeding season when it comes to moorland and rough pasture on islands, and occasionally mainland areas. **Distribution** Breeds in Shetland and Orkney with small numbers in the Outer Hebrides and the north mainland of Scotland. Regular on passage elsewhere, mainly in the autumn.

**Arctic Skua** *Stercorarius parasiticus* 43–47cm (17–18½in) Much more slender built than Great and, unlike that species, occurs in two colour phases together with a variety of intermediates. The central tail feathers are not elongated in immatures. **Flight** Graceful and hawk-like. Very agile when pursuing other seabirds, like the Kittiwake and terns, in order to force them to drop or disgorge their last meal on which it then feeds. **Voice** A wailing 'ki-aow' at the breeding colonies. **Habitat** Similar to Great. **Distribution** Similar to Great though some breed south to the Inner Hebrides. Seen off most coasts in autumn as the birds move south.

# Gulls and terns family Laridae

**Great Black-backed Gull** *Larus marinus* 64–69cm (25–27in) Our largest gull, only possibly confused with smaller Lesser Black-backed which has slate, not a black mantle and wings, and yellow not flesh coloured legs. **Flight** Powerful. **Voice** A barking 'aouk'. **Habitat** Rocky coasts and islands; occasionally inland for breeding. Visits estuaries, lakes and rivers in winter. **Distribution** Breeds around much of Great Britain and Ireland except for the east coast between the Forth and the Isle of Wight; more widespread in winter with immigration from the continent.

**Lesser Black-backed Gull** *Larus fuscus* 53cm (21in) Smaller and more slender built than Great Black-backed. **Flight** Powerful, usually with much gliding. **Voice** A loud 'kiaow-kiaow'. **Habitat** Breeds on islands, occasionally on the mainland coast and not infrequently on inland moors, sometimes in huge colonies. **Distribution** Mainly a summer visitor, mostly breeding in the west and north; passage visitor elsewhere with many more now wintering.

Great Skua

Arctic Skua
dark phase

Arctic Skua
light phase

Lesser Black-backed Gull

Great Black-backed Gull

**Herring Gull** *Larus argentatus* 56cm (22in) The same size as Lesser Black-backed but more stockily built; immatures cannot be separated in their first year or so. **Flight** Powerful, the bird being a master glider in up-draughts above cliffs or when following a ship. **Voice** Varied, but a loud 'kyow-kyow' is most frequently used. **Habitat** Catholic, breeding almost as frequently on low shores as on cliffs; some inland colonies while others nest on roof-tops in coastal towns. Frequent visitor to inland areas and is readily attracted to rubbish dumps, poultry farms and the like. **Distribution** Resident, breeding on virtually all coasts with the smallest numbers in south-east England.

**Common Gull** *Larus canus* 41cm (16in) Rather like a small Herring, but size differences immediately apparent when the two are seen together. Bill shorter and less stout with no red spot near the tip. Legs greenish yellow in contrast to the flesh colour of the larger species. **Flight** Similar to Herring. **Voice** A shrill mewing 'kee-ya'. **Habitat** Breeds mainly inland on moorlands and on islands in lakes. When on the coast it usually chooses fairly level ground but can also be discovered on steep grassy slopes. **Distribution** Breeds mainly in Scotland and Ireland with a handful of pairs in England and Wales. Numerous winter visitor to all areas.

**Black-headed Gull** *Larus ridibundus* 35–38cm (14–15in) Adults in summer plumage with their chocolate brown hood are unmistakable; the red bill and legs are also conspicuous. In late summer the hood is lost, apart from a dark smudge behind the eye, and not regained until the following spring. **Flight** Buoyant and in all plumages a pure white leading edge to the wing is visible. **Voice** A harsh 'kwarr'. **Habitat** Breeds at a variety of inland sites—gravel pits, sewage farms and pools—while on the coast low islands and the fringes of lagoons are chosen. In winter ranges widely inland while it is also numerous on estuaries and sheltered coasts. **Distribution** Breeds throughout much of Great Britain and Ireland, some colonies having long histories while others are short-lived due to habitat changes. More widely distributed in winter.

**Kittiwake** *Rissa tridactyla* 41cm (16in) At first glance rather like a more slender Common Gull, but has much shorter black legs. **Flight** Buoyant, at times swift, the black wing-tips lack the white spots of some other gulls. **Voice** A screaming 'kitt-ee-wake'. **Habitat** Breeds mainly on sea cliffs though harbour walls and warehouses used in a few areas. **Distribution** Breeds on most suitable coastlines, dispersing out to sea in winter.

**Herring Gull** summer

**Herring Gull** winter

**Herring Gull** juvenile

**Common Gull**

winter

summer

**Black-headed Gull**

adult

juvenile

**Kittiwake**

**Black Tern** *Chlidonias niger* 24cm (9½in) Unmistakable in summer plumage; in winter the forehead, neck and underparts are white with a dark 'shoulder' mark extending from the wings. **Flight** Buoyant, frequently hovering just above the water surface. **Voice** A squeaky 'kik-kik'. **Habitat** In breeding season wet marshes and fens; frequents inland waters as well as the coast when on passage. **Distribution** Summer visitor, breeding only in Cambridgeshire, but regular on passage north to central Scotland.

**Common Tern** *Sterna hirundo* 35cm (14in) One of our most graceful seabirds having long wings and tail streamers. In summer the orange-red bill has a distinct, though variable black tip. **Flight** Buoyant, but has deliberate wing-beats. **Voice** A high-pitched 'kee-yah'. **Habitat** Breeds on shingle banks, coastal lagoons and inland on rivers, lakes and gravel pits. **Distribution** Summer visitor, breeding mainly in southern areas, though virtually none in south-west England and south Wales.

**Arctic Tern** *Sterna paradisaea* 35cm (14in) Very similar to Common, though the black tip is absent or much reduced on the blood red bill. **Flight** Similar to Common. **Voice** A whistling 'kee-kee'. **Habitat** Coastal with rather few breeding any distance inland. **Distribution** Breeds mainly in northern England, Scotland and Ireland; regular elsewhere on passage.

**Roseate Tern** *Sterna dougallii* 38cm (15in) Much whiter plumage and longer tail streamers than the previous two species. **Flight** Extremely buoyant with shallow wing-beats. **Voice** A gutteral 'aaak'. **Habitat** Breeds only on the coast, generally choosing rocky islets. **Distribution** Breeds at a limited number of colonies mainly around the Irish Sea; also in north-east England and eastern Scotland. Rare on passage elsewhere though probably overlooked.

**Little Tern** *Sterna albifrons* 23–25cm (9–10in) Our smallest tern and the only one having yellow legs and a black-tipped yellow bill. **Flight** Rapid wing-beats. **Voice** A rasping 'kik-kik' or 'kyik'. **Habitat** Breeds mainly on open beaches rarely occurring inland. **Distribution.** Summer visitor, breeding on most suitable coasts with the greatest number in south-east England.

**Sandwich Tern** *Sterna sandvicensis* 38–43cm (15–17in) Heavier built than other terns. **Flight** More gull-like than other terns. **Voice** A grating 'kirrick'. **Habitat** Breeds on sand-dunes, saltings and shingle. **Distribution** Summer visitor, breeding at a scattering of colonies on most coasts.

**Black Tern**
summer

**Black Tern**
winter

**Common Tern**
summer

**Common Tern**
winter

**Arctic Tern**

**Roseate Tern**

**Sandwich Tern**

**Little Tern**

**Fulmar** *Fulmarus glacialis* (family Procellariidae) 47cm (18½in) Rather gull-like but with a more stocky build, large head, thick neck and yellow bill with characteristic tubed nostril at its base. Ungainly on land, rarely leaving the vicinity of the nest. **Flight** Wings narrower than a gull's, not angled and lacking the black tips. Glides over the sea occasionally beating wings for a few yards. Soars in the up-draught along cliff faces. **Voice** Various chuckling and cackling sounds. **Habitat** Pelagic, coming ashore to breed, mainly on cliff coasts. **Distribution** Breeds virtually all round the coast of Great Britain where there are suitable sites. Absent from its nest sites only during the late autumn and early winter.

# Auks family Alcidae

**Razorbill** *Alca torda* 41cm (16in) Black upperparts; broad bill and stocky build. Throat and cheeks are white in winter and in immature plumages. **Flight** Fast with rapidly whirring wings, usually low over the sea. **Voice** A growling 'aaarr'. **Habitat** Breeds on cliff coasts, usually amongst boulder scree or on broken cliffs. **Distribution** Breeding colonies situated irregularly along most suitable coastlines. In late autumn birds leave colonies, but many remain in inshore waters throughout the winter.

**Guillemot** *Uria aalge* 42cm (16½in) More slender than Razorbill. A 'bridled' form occurs in small numbers and breeds with normal form. **Flight** Flies fast with whirring wings. **Voice** A trumpeting 'arrra'. **Habitat** Breeds on cliff coasts; in suitable areas immense colonies have been established. **Distribution** Similar to Razorbill; the largest colonies are in Scotland. A dispersal through inshore waters during the winter with birds returning sporadically to the colonies from November onwards.

**Black Guillemot** *Cepphus grylle* 34cm (13½in) When on land adopts a sloping rather than an upright stance. **Flight** Similar to Guillemot. **Voice** A thin reedy 'peeeeee'. **Habitat** Low rocky coasts with caves, crevices and boulders among which the birds nest, never in large colonies. **Distribution** Resident breeding from Shetland southwards to the Solway, but normally not south of the Moray Firth on the east coast. Well distributed in Ireland and the Isle of Man with a few pairs in north-west England and north Wales.

**Puffin** *Fratercula arctica* 30cm (12in) Easily distinguished by large and brightly coloured bills. Immatures have a small grey bill. **Flight** Dumpy outline and rapid wing-beats. **Voice** At the colonies a growling 'aarr'. **Habitat** Breeds mainly on remote islands and inaccessible mainland cliffs with steep grass slopes. **Distribution** Summer visitor to northern and western coasts.

Fulmar

Razorbill

bridled form

Guillemot

winter

summer

Black Guillemot

Puffin

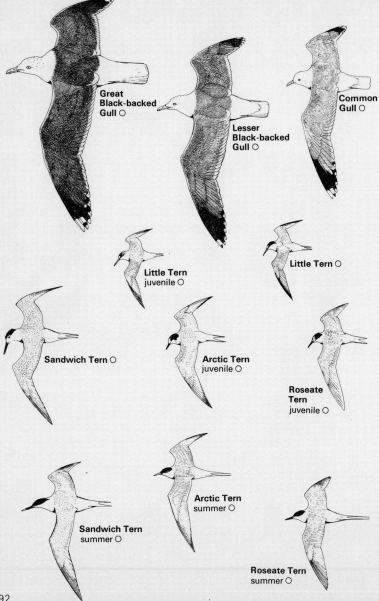

*Seabirds in flight. (Birds with the same accompanying symbol are to the same scale. Those without a symbol are not to scale.)*

**Great Black-backed Gull** ○

**Lesser Black-backed Gull** ○

**Common Gull** ○

**Little Tern** juvenile ○

**Little Tern** ○

**Sandwich Tern** ○

**Arctic Tern** juvenile ○

**Roseate Tern** juvenile ○

**Sandwich Tern** summer ○

**Arctic Tern** summer ○

**Roseate Tern** summer ○

**Gannet** juvenile ○

**Gannet** sub-adult ○

**Cormorant**

**Shag**

**Razorbill** ○

**Guillemot** ○

**Black Guillemot** ○

# Doves, pigeons family Columbidae

**Stock Dove** *Columba oenas* 33cm (13in) Smaller and darker than Woodpigeon and lacking any white markings. **Flight** Rapid, the grey rump and two broken black wing-bars being noticeable. **Voice** A gruff 'oo-roo-oo'. **Habitat** Breeds in holes in trees, particularly old timber; also ruins, cliffs and crags, not infrequently in old rabbit burrows. Feeds on open ground. **Distribution** Resident, breeding north to central and eastern Scotland.

**Rock Dove** *Columba livia* 33cm (13in) Similar to Stock but easily distinguished on the wing. **Flight** Has a striking white rump. **Voice** 'Oo-roo-coo'. **Habitat** Rocky coasts with caves. **Distribution** Occurs only in isolated western and northern areas; elsewhere the population has been much infiltrated by domestic stock. Feral birds often closely resemble the original wild type.

**Woodpigeon** *Columba palumbus* 41cm (16in) Our largest pigeon, adults having a conspicuous white neck patch bordered with glossy green. **Flight** Dashes away noisily when flushed showing a broad white wing-band. **Voice** 'Coo-coo-coo'. **Habitat** Chiefly in agricultural areas with numerous trees; also occurs in the urban zone and in some coastal districts. **Distribution** Resident, occurs in all areas.

**Turtle Dove** *Streptopelia turtur* 27cm (11in) Strikingly rufous upper-parts with a black tail edged with white; a black and white patch on the side of the neck. **Flight** Rather flicking wing-beats while the black tail edged white easily discerned. Noticeably pale underparts. **Voice** A purring 'roor-rrr'. **Habitat** Woodlands, copses, large gardens and thick hedgerows. **Distribution** Summer visitor, breeding mainly in the south, but occurs regularly on passage elsewhere.

**Collared Dove** *Streptopelia decaocto* 32cm (12½in) Much more uniformly coloured than smaller Turtle, and has a narrow black half-collar. **Flight** Direct and swift. **Voice** A noisy 'coo-cooooo-coo'. **Habitat** Usually close to human habitation, especially where there are tall trees for nesting. **Distribution** Resident, now breeding throughout much of Great Britain and Ireland.

**Cuckoo** *Cuculus canorus* (family Cuculidae) 33cm (13in) A grey, slender built bird with a long tail. **Flight** Usually low and hurried and terminating in a long glide. Looks not unlike small hawk or falcon. Wings pointed. **Voice** Unmistakable call of the male; females have a bubbling chuckle. **Habitat** Varies from woodlands to moorland and treeless islands. **Distribution** Summer visitor, arriving during late April and breeding throughout Great Britain and Ireland.

Stock Dove

Rock Dove

Woodpigeon

Turtle Dove

Collared Dove

Cuckoo

# Owls families Tytonidae and Strigidae

**Barn Owl** *Tyto alba* 34cm (13½in) A pale owl which in the half light at dusk, or when seen briefly in car headlights, looks all-white. **Flight** Slow flapping, at times wavering on rounded wings. **Voice** Wild shrieks, various hissing and snoring noises. **Habitat** Usually agricultural country, but may occur in other open country. **Distribution** Breeds in small numbers in most areas, though not north-west Scotland.

**Snowy Owl** *Nyctea scandiaca* 53–60cm (21–24in) Unmistakable with its huge size, white plumage with variable brown or blackish bars. **Flight** Chiefly diurnal; more Buzzard- than owl-like with frequent glides. **Voice** Normally silent except when breeding. **Habitat** Moorland with rocky knolls. **Distribution** Breeds only on RSPB reserve at Fetlar (Shetlands), but birds seen in summer in several other northern areas. Occasionally wanders further south, especially in winter.

**Little Owl** *Athene noctua* 22cm (8½in) Small size and rather squat flat-headed appearance with bright yellow eyes. Has frequent bobbing action and regularly hunts by day. **Flight** Low, rapid with deep undulations. **Habitat** Varied, but usually in timbered agricultural areas. **Distribution** Resident, breeding north to the border counties; absent other than as a vagrant in Ireland.

**Tawny Owl** *Strix aluco* 38cm (15in) Mainly nocturnal and usually only seen by day at a roosting place where its black eyes and lack of ear-tufts prevent confusion with Long-eared. **Flight** Large head and broad, rounded wings prominent. **Voice** Familiar hooting 'song' and a loud 'kee-wick'. **Habitat** Mainly woodland areas including city parks. **Distribution** Resident, breeding throughout Great Britain except the far north-west and in Ireland.

**Long-eared Owl** *Asio otus* 45cm (13½in) Nocturnal, seldom seen except at regular winter roosts. Has a slim shape, orange eyes and elongated 'ear' tufts. **Flight** Wings and tail longer than Tawny. **Voice** A low 'oo-oo-oo'. **Habitat** Woodland, especially conifers, but hunts in open country. **Distribution** Widely distributed, though local in all areas including Ireland.

**Short-eared Owl** *Asio flammeus* 38cm (15in) Regularly hunts by day, and when at rest adopts a slanting rather than upright inclination. **Flight** Long wings and rather harrier-like movements. **Habitat** Open country. **Distribution** Resident, breeding mainly in northern and western England; a few pairs in eastern districts and throughout Scotland. Regular in winter on the coast elsewhere.

Barn Owl

Snowy Owl

Little Owl

Tawny Owl

Long-eared Owl

Short-eared Owl

**Nightjar** *Caprimulgus europaeus* (family Caprimulgidae) 27cm (10½in) Crepuscular and rarely seen by day, its finely patterned plumage being an excellent woodland floor camouflage. **Flight** Light, floating, with acrobatic dashes after flying insects. White wing-patches on male. **Voice** A loud nocturnal 'churring'. **Habitat** Woodland, bracken hillsides, dunes and moorland. **Distribution** Decreasing summer visitor, widespread but local.

**Swift** *Apus apus* (family Apodidae) 16·5cm (6½in) Long scythe-like wings and dark plumage distinguish it from swallows. **Flight** Vigorous and wheeling. **Voice** Mainly a loud screaming. **Habitat** Encountered in all types of habitat but for breeding requires holes in buildings; occasionally cliff crevices. **Distribution** Summer visitor in most areas.

**Kingfisher** *Alcedo atthis* (family Alcedinidae) 16·5cm (6½in) Unmistakable bright plumage. **Flight** Rapid and usually low. Hovers when fishing. **Voice** A piping 'chee'. **Habitat** Mainly slow flowing rivers and streams, often moving to the coast in winter. **Distribution** Widespread resident except north to central Scotland.

**Green Woodpecker** *Picus viridis* (family Picidae) 32cm (12½in) Largest and immediately identifiable woodpecker. **Flight** Alternately rising with a few wing-beats and dipping with wings closed. **Voice** A loud, rapid 'laughing' call. **Habitat** Mainly deciduous woodland but roams to open country feeding mostly on the ground. **Distribution** Resident north to central Scotland, but absent from Ireland.

**Great Spotted Woodpecker** *Dendrocopos major* 23cm (9in) Strikingly patterned black and white with red undertail coverts. **Flight** Similar to Green. **Voice** A loud 'tchick'; also in spring a 'drumming' noise produced by rapidly striking a dead branch. **Habitat** Woodland. **Distribution** Resident in most areas, but only a casual visitor to Ireland.

**Lesser Spotted Woodpecker** *Dendrocopos minor* 14·5cm (5¾in) Small size and barred back and wings distinctive. **Flight** Similar to Green. **Voice** A shrill 'pee-pee-pee'; also 'drums'. **Habitat** Woodland. **Distribution** Widespread resident, absent from Scotland and Ireland.

**Wryneck** *Jynx torquilla* 16·5cm (6½in) Looks more like a grey-brown passerine than a woodpecker. **Flight** Slow and undulating. **Voice** A shrill 'quee-quee-quee'. **Habitat** Woods, open parkland, orchards and gardens. **Distribution** Rare summer visitor, almost extinct in south-east England, but a few pairs recently in Scotland. Regular in small numbers on autumn passage, mostly on the east coast.

Nightjar

Swift

Kingfisher

Green Woodpecker

Great Spotted Woodpecker

Lesser Spotted Woodpecker

Wryneck

# Larks, Swallow and martins

**Woodlark** *Lullula arborea* (family Alaudidae) 15cm (6in) Shorter tailed than larger Skylark and has conspicuous white eye-stripes. **Flight** Normal flight undulating, also has a circular song flight at a constant height. **Voice** Melodious, though less powerful than Skylark; call note 'titloo-eet'. **Habitat** Varied, but with scattered trees and scrub. **Distribution** Resident, breeding locally in southern England and Wales.

**Skylark** *Alauda arvensis* 17·5cm (7in) Generally streaky brown, slightly crested with white outer tail. **Flight** Strong and slightly undulating, performs the well-known song-flight. **Voice** A sustained song often from great height. Flight note 'chirrup'. **Habitat** Open country. **Distribution** Common resident throughout Great Britain and Ireland.

**Shorelark** *Eremophila alpestris* 16·5cm (6½in) Bold patterning on head, duller in winter and not so pronounced in females and immatures, distinguishes it from other larks. **Flight** Similar to Skylark. **Voice** A shrill 'tsissup'. **Habitat** Beaches, saltings and stubble fields near the coast. **Distribution** Winter visitor, mainly to the east coast south of Yorkshire; occasional elsewhere.

**Swallow** *Hirundo rustica* (family Hirundinidae) 19cm (7½in) Easily recognized and distinguished from other hirundines by its long tail streamers, chestnut throat and forehead, though these features are less pronounced in young birds. **Flight** Graceful and aerobatic; normally only settles on the ground when collecting nest material. **Voice** A rapid twitter. **Habitat** Open country where buildings are available for nest sites and usually close to water. **Distribution** Summer visitor throughout Great Britain and Ireland.

**House Martin** *Delichon urbica* 12·5cm (5in) Entire underparts white, contrasting with the mainly blue-black upperparts with a white rump. In some places large numbers nest close together. **Flight** Often flies higher than Swallow. **Voice** A clear 'chirrp'. **Habitat** Open country; mostly nesting on buildings but also uses cliff faces. **Distribution** Summer visitor throughout much of Great Britain and Ireland.

**Sand Martin** *Riparia riparia* 12cm (4¾in) Smaller than Swallow with brown upperparts and a distinct brown chest band. **Flight** Rather more fluttering and erratic than Swallow. **Voice** A harsh 'tchrrip'. **Habitat** Open country where river banks, cuttings and sand and gravel pits provide suitable nesting places, sometimes for large colonies. **Distribution** Summer visitor to much of Great Britain and Ireland; scarce in the extreme north-west.

Woodlark

Skylark

Shorelark ♂

Swallow

House Martin

Sand Martin

# Crows family Corvidae

**Raven** *Corvus corax* 64cm (25in) Our largest crow, having a massive bill and shaggy throat feathers. **Flight** Powerful; often aerobatic, when overhead the wedge-shaped tail may be seen. **Voice** A deep 'kronking'. **Habitat** Mainly coastal and upland regions. **Distribution** Resident in western and northern areas.

**Carrion Crow** *Corvus corone* 45cm (18½in) All-black plumage. The Hooded Crow, with grey mantle and underparts, replaces the Carrion Crow in Ireland and the Scottish Isles, and outnumbers the Carrion Crow in north Scotland and the Isle of Man. In parts of the Highlands the two forms interbreed. **Flight** Regular wing-beats. **Voice** A croaking 'kraah'. **Habitat** Almost ubiquitous. **Distribution** Resident throughout Great Britain and Ireland.

**Rook** *Corvus frugilegus* 46cm (18in) Adult easily separated from Carrion Crow by the pale greyish patch of bare skin around the base of the bill and the baggy thigh feathers. **Flight** Direct with steady wing-beats; wheels around rookery. **Voice** A harsh 'caw' but has variety of other calls. **Habitat** Agricultural areas with tall trees for colonial nesting. **Distribution** Resident in most areas.

**Jackdaw** *Corvus monedula* 33cm (13in) Its small size, grey nape and ear coverts distinguish this species from the larger crows. **Flight** Faster wing-beats than Rook and Carrion Crow. **Voice** A high pitched 'chak'. **Habitat** Open country having ruins, cliffs and old timber in which the birds nest. **Distribution** Resident throughout Great Britain and Ireland.

**Magpie** *Pica pica* 46cm (18in) Unmistakable with pied plumage and long (up to 25cm, 10in) tail. **Flight** Rather slow though with quite rapid wing-beats. **Voice** A harsh 'chak-chak-chak'. **Habitat** Chiefly farmland but increasingly suburban; usually nests in tall hedges. **Distribution** Resident north to central Scotland; locally in the eastern Highlands.

**Jay** *Garrulus glandarius* 34cm (13½in) Brightly patterned though surprisingly well camouflaged in woodland. **Flight** Rather jerky with rounded wings; a conspicuous white rump. **Voice** A harsh 'skraaak'. **Habitat** Mainly woodland. **Distribution** Resident north to central Scotland but absent from some lowland counties. In Ireland it is absent from the far west and local in parts of its range.

**Chough** *Pyrrhocorax pyrrhocorax* 39·5cm (15½in) More slender than Jackdaw and having a curved red bill and legs. **Voice** A high-pitched 'kyow'. **Habitat** Rocky coasts, but inland in some mountainous areas. **Distribution** Resident, restricted to parts of Ireland, Wales, the Isle of Man and the south Inner Hebrides.

Raven

Carrion Crow

Rook

Jackdaw

Magpie

Jay

Chough

# Tits family Paridae

**Great Tit** *Parus major* 14cm (5½in) Our largest tit and a familiar garden bird, with a broad black band down the centre of its bright yellow underparts. **Flight** Usually of short duration from tree to tree; undulating may rise high over longer distances. **Voice** Main song a loud repeated 'teacher, teacher'; a wide variety of other notes. **Habitat** Woodlands, gardens and hedgerows. **Distribution** Resident in all areas.

**Blue Tit** *Parus caeruleus* 11·5cm (4½in) Bright blue cap marks it out from other tits. Yellow underparts. **Flight** Similar to Great, but weaker, more fluttering. **Voice** Main note a scolding 'tsee-tsee-tsee'. **Habitat** Similar to Great, though regularly wanders to reedbeds and wasteland in winter. **Distribution** Resident throughout Great Britain and Ireland except Orkney and Shetland.

**Coal Tit** *Parus ater* 11·5cm (4½in) The white nape-patch and double white wing-bars distinguish it from other tits of the same size. Often moves in Treecreeper fashion on the trunks of trees. **Flight** As for Blue. **Voice** A piping 'tsu-i' and a rather Goldcrest-like 'tsee-tsee-tsee'. Song has repeated double note pattern of Great, but is thinner and faster. **Habitat** Mainly woodland, especially conifers. **Distribution** Resident in all areas except Orkney and Shetland.

**Crested Tit** *Parus cristatus* 11·5cm (4½in) Speckled black and white crest separates it from all other species of this size. **Flight** As for Blue. **Voice** A low purring 'choor-r-r'. **Habitat** Coniferous woodland especially mature Scots pine. **Distribution** Resident, restricted to the eastern Highlands of Scotland.

**Marsh Tit** *Parus palustris* 11·5cm (4½in) Combination of black cap and plain brown upperparts distinguishes Marsh from all others, except Willow. See Willow for differences. **Flight** As for Blue. **Voice** Various calls; a loud 'pitcheew' positively identifies this species. **Habitat** Typically deciduous woods, especially oak, also hedgerows. **Distribution** Resident in England and Wales, but absent from Scotland (except Berwick) and Ireland.

**Willow Tit** *Parus montanus* 11·5cm (4½in) Differs from Marsh in having a matt rather than glossy crown, and a pale patch in the closed secondaries. These distinctions are often difficult to see, and young or worn Marsh and Willows may look very similar. The safest clues are the distinctive 'pitcheew' note of Marsh and the repeated nasal note of Willow. **Flight** As for Great. **Voice** Various calls of which a harsh nasal 'dzee-dzee-dzee-dzee' is typical. **Habitat** Wood, copses, hedgerows, but a preference for damp areas where nest holes are excavated in rotten trunks and branches. **Distribution** Similar to Marsh though extends into south-west Scotland.

Great Tit

Blue Tit

Coal Tit

Crested Tit

Marsh Tit

Willow Tit

**Long-tailed Tit** *Aegithalos caudatus* (family Aegithalidae) 14cm (5½in) A small, black, white and pinkish bird with a tail over half its total length. Often remains in family parties in autumn and winter, sometimes mixing with other tits, Goldcrests and Treecreepers. **Flight** Rather laboured and undulating. **Voice** Typical notes include a repeated, short, hard 'tut' and a thin 'zee-zee-zee'. **Habitat** Hedgerows, bushy heaths, scrub and woodland. **Distribution** Resident throughout Great Britain and Ireland, except for the extreme north of Scotland.

**Nuthatch** *Sitta europaea* (family Sittidae) 14cm (5½in) Blue-grey upperparts and mainly buffish chestnut underparts. Has a long straight bill and surprising agility when ascending or descending tree-trunks. **Flight** Usually short between trees. **Voice** Includes a loud ringing 'chwit-chwit' and a repeated clear piping note. **Habitat** Woodland or parkland and gardens with large trees. **Distribution** Resident in most of England and Wales, but absent from Scotland and Ireland.

**Treecreeper** *Certhia familiaris* (family Certhiidae) 12·5cm (5in) Upperparts streaked brown in contrast with the white underparts. Long curved bill used for extracting insects and spiders from bark crevices as it climbs trunks. Often moves through woods climbing up and around one tree, then flying down to the base of the next. **Flight** Rather tit-like. **Voice** A thin high-pitched 'tsee'. **Habitat** As for Nuthatch. **Distribution** Resident in most areas.

**Wren** *Troglodytes troglodytes* (family Troglodytidae) 9·5cm (3¾in) One of our most familiar birds with russet brown plumage and a short, usually erect tail. **Flight** Straight, with whirring wings. **Voice** A hard scolding 'tic-tic-tic', and a loud, shrill hurried song. **Habitat** Low cover in a great variety of country. **Distribution** Resident throughout Great Britain and Ireland.

**Dipper** *Cinclus cinclus* (family Cinclidae) 18cm (7in) Has the shape of a giant Wren, with a conspicuous white throat and chestnut belly. Wades, and can feed under water, either swimming or walking on the bottom. **Flight** Rapid and usually low. **Voice** A metallic 'clink'. **Habitat** Fast-flowing streams and rivers. **Distribution** Resident in western and northern areas.

**Bearded Reedling** *Panurus biarmicus* (family Timaliidae) 16·5cm (6½in) Mainly tawny brown, long-tailed, males having conspicuous head markings. **Flight** Rather laboured and undulating on whirring wings. **Voice** A metallic 'tching-tching'. **Habitat** Large reedbeds for breeding, though in winter it may occur in much smaller areas. **Distribution** Resident which has recently spread from East Anglia to nest in several southern counties, and suitable sites elsewhere.

Long-tailed Tit

Nuthatch

Treecreeper

Wren

Dipper

Bearded Reedling

# Thrushes, chats family Turdidae

**Mistle Thrush** *Turdus viscivorus* 27cm (10$\frac{1}{2}$in) Larger and greyer than Song with bolder breast spots, white underwing and tips to outer tail. **Flight** Strong and level despite frequent closures of the wings. **Voice** A harsh 'churring', and a loud song of short phrases, rather like Blackbird in tone. **Habitat** Woods, farmland, parks and gardens. **Distribution** Resident, breeding in all areas.

**Fieldfare** *Turdus pilaris* 25·5cm (10in) Its grey head, neck and rump, and chestnut back are distinctive. **Flight** Similar to slightly larger Mistle Thrush. **Voice** A harsh repeated 'chack-chack'. **Habitat** Open country with hedges and copses of berry-bearing shrubs. **Distribution** Winter visitor but in recent years has nested several times in Scotland and the northern Isles and exceptionally in northern England.

**Song Thrush** *Turdus philomelos* 23cm (9in) Smaller and browner than Mistle, and more buffish on the flanks. **Flight** Fast and direct. **Voice** Song is a series of repeated musical phrases, call note a thin 'sipp'. **Habitat** Varied, where there is enough cover for nesting, often close to human habitation. **Distribution** Resident throughout Great Britain and Ireland.

**Redwing** *Turdus iliacus* 21cm (8$\frac{1}{4}$in) Darker brown than Song Thrush with a pale eye-stripe and reddish flanks. **Flight** As for Song but reddish flanks and axillaries may be distinguished. **Voice** A thin 'seeip', often heard from migrants overhead at night. **Habitat** Breeds in woodland; frequents open and wooded country in winter. **Distribution** Chiefly a widespread winter visitor, but in recent years has increasingly nested in Scotland.

**Ring Ouzel** *Turdus torquatus* 24cm (9$\frac{1}{2}$in) Rather like Blackbird but both sexes have a white gorget on the breast (less obvious in female) and a pale wing-patch. **Flight** Rapid and direct. **Voice** A loud 'tac-tac-tac', and a loud, clear, but limited song. **Habitat** Breeds mainly on mountain and moorland, particularly where there are patches of scrub; often seen near the coast when on passage. **Distribution** Summer visitor in western and northern areas.

**Blackbird** *Turdus merula* 25cm (10in) One of our most striking and well-known birds, the female being browner. **Flight** Rather direct, though wavering over short distances. **Voice** A rich fluty song, an anxious 'tchook', and the familiar screaming chatter alarm cry. **Habitat** Varied, providing there is enough cover for nesting. **Distribution** Resident throughout Great Britain and Ireland.

Mistle Thrush

Fieldfare

Redwing

Song Thrush

Blackbird ♂

Blackbird ♀

Ring Ouzel ♂ ♀

**Wheatear** *Oenanthe oenanthe* 14·5cm (5¼in) An alert and active bird. **Flight** Low and direct. Regardless of sex or age the white rump and tail sides are immediately visible. **Voice** A grating 'chack-chack' and a short, warbling song. **Habitat** Moorland, heaths, downs and coastal turf. **Distribution** Widespread summer visitor in all areas except central and south-east England.

**Stonechat** *Saxicola torquata* 12·5cm (5in) A striking species easily located as it generally perches in conspicuous positions. Quick movements, flicks tail and wings. **Flight** Low with fast wing-beats, showing dark tail and white wing-patches. **Voice** A repeated harsh 'tsak-tsak' resembling small pebbles being knocked together. **Habitat** Special liking for gorse; commons, coastal headlands, rough hillsides and heaths. **Distribution** Resident mainly in western and northern coastal counties.

**Whinchat** *Saxicola rubetra* 12·5cm (5in) Similar in habits to Stonechat. Pale eye-stripe is a useful distinguishing mark. **Flight** Jerky, with white showing on the sides of the tail close to its base. **Voice** A grating 'tic-tic', a liquid 'tu', and a short warbling song. **Habitat** Rough grassland, heaths and moors, young conifer plantations. **Distribution** Summer visitor to much of Great Britain, but only local in Ireland and south-east England.

**Redstart** *Phoenicurus phoenicurus* 14cm (5½in) An active species which constantly quivers its reddish tail in an up-and-down motion. **Flight** Reddish tail striking. **Voice** A Willow Warbler-like 'hooeet', and a liquid 'tooick'. Brief musical song with jangling finish. **Habitat** Breeds in deciduous woodland. **Distribution** Summer visitor to most of Great Britain though rare in Ireland.

**Black Redstart** *Phoenicurus ochruros* 14cm (5½in) The black or greyish underparts distinguish it from Redstart. **Flight** Reddish tail conspicuous. **Voice** Scolding 'tucc-tucc', and a quick warbly song. **Habitat** Buildings, especially power stations and factory areas, cliffs and quarries. **Distribution** A scarce summer visitor, breeding mainly in south-east England; some overwinter. Regular passage migrant on east and south coasts.

**Nightingale** *Luscinia megarhynchos* 16·5cm (6½in) A skulking bird with all-brown upperparts and a rufous tail. **Flight** Usually low with tail conspicuous. **Voice** Loud, rich and varied song, pausing between phrases. Sings by day and night; alarm notes harsh and grating. **Habitat** Mainly woodland with thick undergrowth. **Distribution** Summer visitor, mainly south and east of a line from Dorset to the Wash.

**Robin** *Erithacus rubecula* 14cm (5½in) Adults unmistakable; speckled immatures, however, lack the red breast. **Flight** Usually low. **Voice** A loud warbly song and a 'tic-tic' note. **Habitat** Varied, where cover is available. **Distribution** Resident, breeding in all areas except Shetland.

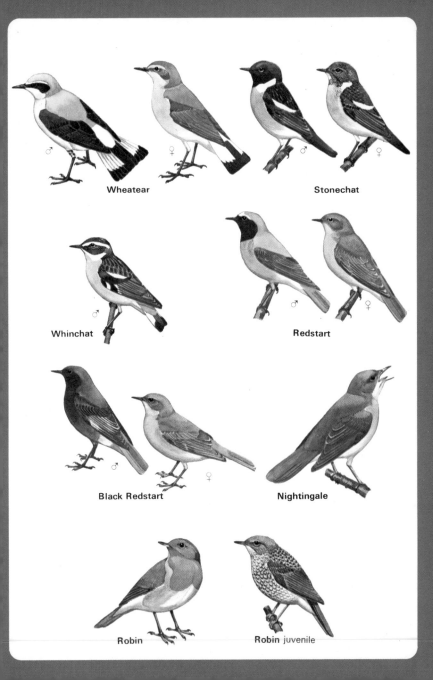

Wheatear

Stonechat

Whinchat

Redstart

Black Redstart

Nightingale

Robin

Robin juvenile

# Warblers family Sylviidae

**Grasshopper Warbler** *Locustella naevia* 12·5cm (5in) Difficult to see, slips through cover. Has strongly streaked brown upperparts and a rounded tail. **Flight** Usually of short duration, the bird quickly seeking cover. **Voice** A characteristic reeling song, often heard after dark as well as by day. **Habitat** Varies from marshland to heaths and young conifer plantations, but always with thick undergrowth. **Distribution** Summer visitor to all counties except parts of north Scotland and the Isles.

**Reed Warbler** *Acrocephalus scirpaceus* 12·5cm (5in) Uniform brown upperparts and light buff underparts. No distinct eye-stripe. **Flight** Usually of short duration with a spread tail. **Voice** A low 'churr' and a deliberate song of repeated, mostly harsh, sounds. **Habitat** Reedbeds. **Distribution** Summer visitor to England and Wales, though absent or local in the west and north.

**Sedge Warbler** *Acrocephalus schoenobaenus* 12·5cm (5in) Has boldly streaked upperparts and a conspicuous whitish eye-stripe. **Flight** Tail is spread during short flights, while the tawny rump is apparent. **Voice** A loud 'tuc-tuc', and mixed 'churrings'. Song lacks the steady rhythm of Reed Warbler, is faster, more varied, sometimes imitating other birds. **Habitat** Mainly thick vegetation near water. **Distribution** Summer visitor to most of Great Britain and Ireland.

**Blackcap** *Sylvia atricapilla* 14cm (5½in) Male's black, and female's red-brown, caps are distinctive. Both have grey-brown upperparts and pale underparts. **Flight** Usually reluctant to fly any distance and quickly retires into cover. **Voice** A distinctive scolding 'tchack', while the song is easy, rich, and tuneful. Also has a faster sub-song, much like the song of Garden Warbler. **Habitat** Generally wooded areas, large gardens and overgrown hedges. **Distribution** Summer visitor, breeding in Great Britain except the far north, less commonly in Ireland, except the north-west. Has in recent years shown an increasing tendency to overwinter and may come to bird tables.

**Garden Warbler** *Sylvia borin* 14cm (5½in) Plumage uniform and lacking any distinctive features. Rather plump with a round head and short bill. **Flight** Similar to Blackcap. **Voice** Song is faster and more uniform than Blackcap's song, but similar to Blackcap's sub-song. Calls low and harsh. **Habitat** Woods, bushy commons, heaths, large gardens and parks. **Distribution** Summer visitor, breeding throughout Great Britain, apart from the extreme north-west. In Ireland, extremely local, mainly in the Shannon valley.

Grasshopper Warbler

Reed Warbler

Sedge Warbler

Blackcap ♀

Blackcap ♂

Garden Warbler

**Whitethroat** *Sylvia communis* 14cm (5$\frac{1}{2}$in) Male has a grey cap and cheeks contrasting with a white throat and a rufous patch in the wings. Female has the white throat under a brown head. Tail rather long, white-edged. **Flight** Rather jerky and short, often diving into cover. **Voice** Various scolding notes. Rapid chattering song often delivered during a dancing song flight. **Habitat** Open areas with thick cover of hedgerows, brambles, nettles, scrub or osiers. **Distribution** Summer visitor breeding throughout Great Britain and Ireland.

**Lesser Whitethroat** *Sylvia curruca* 13·5cm (5$\frac{1}{4}$in) Sexes similar, more compact than Whitethroat, having greyer upperparts and a dark patch on the ear coverts. **Flight** As for Whitethroat. **Voice** A rather Blackcap-like 'tchak'. The song is a distinctive fast rattle on one note, usually preceded by a short warble. **Habitat** Similar to Whitethroat but often amongst taller growth. **Distribution** Summer visitor, breeding mainly in south-eastern England, locally elsewhere; absent from Scotland and Ireland.

**Dartford Warbler** *Sylvia undata* 12·5cm (5in) A skulking dark plum-aged bird with a long, often cocked or fanned tail. **Flight** Weak, undulating action with fast wing-beats and a bobbing tail. **Voice** A scolding 'tchir-r' song rather Whitethroat-like. **Habitat** Heath areas with gorse. **Distribution** Resident, breeding in a few southern counties principally Dorset and Hampshire.

**Willow Warbler** *Phylloscopus trochilus* 11cm (4$\frac{1}{4}$in) Plumage some-what more greenish above and yellowish beneath than Chiffchaff, but distinction not clear cut. Legs pale; Chiffchaff's legs are usually dark. **Flight** Rather jerky. **Voice** A gentle 'hoo-eet', and a sweet descending song ending with a flourish. **Habitat** Varied; woods, and more open areas with trees, tall scrub, hedges. **Distribution** Summer visitor, breeding in all counties, except Shetland.

**Chiffchaff** *Phylloscopus collybita* 11cm (4$\frac{1}{4}$in) Best distinguished from Willow by its song. **Flight** As for Willow. **Voice** Song the familiar steadily repeated 'chiff-chaff'; call 'hweet'. **Habitat** More restricted to mature woodland than Willow Warbler. **Distribution** Summer visitor, breeding in most counties, but local in north-east, with a few overwintering.

**Wood Warbler** *Phylloscopus sibilatrix* 12·5cm (5in) Brighter green back than two previous warblers, yellow throat and breast, white belly and marked eye-stripe. **Flight** As for Willow. **Voice** An accelerating trill and a repeated plaintive 'piu'; usual call a similar note uttered singly. **Habitat** Mature woodlands. **Distribution** Summer visitor to most of Britain; rather local in the south-east and extreme north-west, and very local in Ireland.

Whitethroat

Lesser Whitethroat

Dartford Warbler

Willow Warbler

Chiffchaff

Wood Warbler

**Goldcrest** *Regulus regulus* (family Regulidae) 9cm (3½in) Very small and compact, plump and fine-billed. Double white wing-bar, and on adults bright crown. Often mixes with tit flocks outside the breeding season. **Flight** Rather tit-like. **Voice** Call a high, thin 'zee-zee-zee-zee'. Song is high-pitched and short, a repeated double note, followed by a flourish. **Habitat** Typically coniferous woods, local in deciduous areas; many move to hedgerows and scrub in winter. **Distribution** Resident in all counties except Orkney and Shetland.

**Firecrest** *Regulus ignicapillus* 9cm (3½in) Similar build and habits to Goldcrest from which it is best distinguished by the striking head pattern of black and white eye-stripes. Also greener above, whiter below, with a bronzy shade on the sides of the neck. **Flight** As for Goldcrest. **Voice** Call a less high-pitched 'zit'. **Habitat** Breeds in mixed woods, especially with spruce and larch; otherwise in a variety of habitats with trees and bushes. **Distribution** Mainly a passage migrant in England; scarce elsewhere; since 1961 has bred in southern counties; is increasing and spreading.

# Flycatchers family Muscicapidae

**Spotted Flycatcher** *Muscicapa striata* 14cm (5½in) The upright stance, and rapid flights from the same perch after insects immediately identify this bird as a flycatcher. The sexes are similar, mouse-brown with slight streaking on crown and breast. **Flight** Flutters and twists after insects; longer flights are rapid and undulating. **Voice** Main call a Robin-like 'tzee'; song simply a few squeaky notes. **Habitat** Open woodland, gardens, parkland. **Distribution** Summer visitor.

**Pied Flycatcher** *Ficedula hypoleuca* 13cm (5in) The male in summer plumage is a distinctive black and white; females and males in autumn are brown and white. The white wing-patch and outer tail prevent confusion with slightly larger Spotted. **Flight** Unlike that species it rarely returns to the same perch when feeding. Tail is constantly flirted. **Voice** A loud 'whit' and a 'wheet'; song short and pleasing with Redstart-like trill. **Habitat** Well-developed woodland, often along valleys in hilly country. **Distribution** Summer visitor, breeding in western and northern counties to the central Highlands. Occurs in Ireland only whilst on passage, when it is also regular on the English east coast.

**Dunnock** *Prunella modularis* (family Prunellidae) 14·5cm (5¾in) A plump bird with a thin bill, streaked back and grey head and underparts. Usually keeps in or close to cover. Frequently flicks its wings. **Flight** Usually low and over a short distance. **Voice** A shrill 'seep'; song a weak pleasant jingle. **Habitat** Hedgerows, bushy areas, scrub, open woods with undergrowth. **Distribution** Resident throughout Great Britain and Ireland.

Goldcrest

Firecrest

Spotted Flycatcher

Pied Flycatcher

Dunnock

# Pipits, wagtails family Motacillidae

**Meadow Pipit** *Anthus pratensis* 14·5cm (5¾in) Streaked, with a rather long, white-edged tail; spends most of its time on the ground. Rather similar to Tree from which it is best distinguished by song. **Flight** Rather jerky, rising and falling; often sings in climbing flight and 'parachute' descent. **Voice** A thin 'tseep' repeated thin notes becoming more musical and ending in a trill. **Habitat** Rough open country. **Distribution** Resident.

**Tree Pipit** *Anthus trivialis* 15cm (6in) Slightly larger than Meadow, and of a warmer buffish-brown colour, but voice is best distinction. **Flight** Has a song flight whilst descending to a perch, usually in a tree. **Voice** A loud, at times shrill, song. Less hurried, sweeter than Meadow; call a hoarse 'teez'. **Habitat** Heaths, hillsides and commons with scattered trees, woodland glades and edges. **Distribution** Summer visitor, breeding in most areas; not Ireland.

**Rock Pipit** *Anthus spinoletta* 16·5cm (6½in) Larger and darker than the two previous species, with dark legs and dusky, not white, outer tail feathers. **Flight** As for Meadow and has a similar song flight. **Voice** Call note 'tsup', not as thin and squeaky as Meadow. Song resembles Meadow but louder and fuller. **Habitat** Rocky coasts. **Distribution** Resident on all coasts except low-lying eastern ones, though winters there.

**Pied/White Wagtail** *Motacilla alba* 18cm (7in) Contrasting black and white plumage, long slender build and continual tail movements quickly identify this species. The White Wagtail has a pale grey back and rump, but in autumn the races are very similar. **Flight** Undulating. **Voice** A loud 'tchizzik' call, and a twittering song. **Habitat** Open country with buildings, banks, etc., to provide nest sites usually near water. **Distribution** Pied a resident, breeding in all counties; White seen chiefly on passage, occasionally nests in far north.

**Grey Wagtail** *Motacilla cinerea* 18cm (7in) Blue-grey upperparts, yellowish rump and longer tail prevent confusion with Yellow. **Voice** Usual call rather shorter, higher-pitched than other wagtails. **Habitat** Nests usually beside fast-flowing water, spreading to a variety of sites near water in winter. **Distribution** Resident in most counties; local or absent except outside breeding season from eastern England.

**Yellow/Blue-headed Wagtail** *Motacilla flava* 16·5cm (6½in) Shorter tail than Grey and a greenish brown back. **Flight** Undulating. **Voice** A shrill 'tseweeep'; song a simple warble. **Habitat** Lowland meadows, marshland and some heaths, usually near water. **Distribution** Summer visitor, breeding throughout much of England; local or absent elsewhere except on passage. The Blue-headed Wagtail or variants breed very locally in the south-east; occasionally elsewhere.

**Meadow Pipit**

**Tree Pipit**

**Rock Pipit**

**Pied Wagtail**

**White Wagtail**

**Grey Wagtail**
summary

**Yellow Wagtail**

**Blue-headed Wagtail**

**Waxwing** *Bombycilla garrulus* (family Bombycillidae) 18cm (7in) Prominently crested with bright plumage. **Flight** Similar to Starling, and has a grey rump and lower back. **Voice** A trilling 'sirrr'. **Habitat** Associated with berry-bearing shrubs and trees wherever these occur; commons, parks, gardens. **Distribution** Winter visitor, mainly to eastern counties with occasional 'invasions' westwards.

**Red-backed Shrike** *Lanius collurio* (family Laniidae) 17cm (6¾in) Striking plumage and habit of sitting on prominent perches aid identification. **Flight** Rather dipping with pointed wings and a long tail; can hover, and darts about to catch flies. **Voice** A harsh 'chack-chack'. **Habitat** Scrubby commons, bramble patches and thickets. **Distribution** Summer visitor, much decreased in numbers and now only breeding in south-east England.

**Starling** *Sturnus vulgaris* (family Sturnidae) 21·5cm (8½in) One of our best known birds. **Flight** Direct and rapid with frequent glides. **Voice** Common call a harsh descending 'tcheer'. A rather warbly song interspersed with whistles and rattles. Good mimic. **Habitat** From cities to remote coasts. **Distribution** Resident.

**Hawfinch** *Coccothraustes coccothraustes* (family Fringillidae) 18cm (7in) A large finch with a thick neck and bill and secretive habits. **Flight** Rapid wing-beats and undulating. **Voice** An explosive 'tzik'. **Habitat** Mature deciduous woods, gardens and orchards. **Distribution** Resident, breeding locally in England, Wales and southern Scotland; an occasional visitor to Ireland.

**Greenfinch** *Carduelis chloris* 14·5cm (5¾in) A plump greenish bird with yellow wing-patches. **Flight** Slightly undulating, the yellow wing-patches and tail sides being noticeable. **Voice** Usual call a rapid musical twitter, a wheezing 'tswee' from males in spring; the song, a medley of twittering notes, is often delivered in a slow-flapping 'butterfly' flight. **Habitat** All areas with trees and bushes. **Distribution** Resident.

**Goldfinch** *Carduelis carduelis* 12cm (4¾in) The sexes are similarly brightly coloured, the young streaky grey but showing the bold wing and tail patterns. **Flight** Rather dancing with a yellow wing-bar. **Voice** Usual call a repeated liquid note; song a pleasant liquid twittering. **Habitat** Similar to Greenfinch, often feeds on low plants, thistle, etc. **Distribution** Resident, breeding in all counties except for the north and north-west of Scotland.

**Siskin** *Carduelis spinus* 12cm (4¾in) Females are greyer with more streaks beneath and no black on the head. **Flight** Buoyant, with yellow sides to tail, and wing-bar. **Voice** Shrill and twittering calls. **Habitat** Breeds in coniferous woods, spreads in winter to alders and birches, and increasingly, gardens. **Distribution** Resident, nesting mainly in Scotland; locally further south. Widespread in winter.

Waxwing ♀

Red-backed Shrike ♂

Red-backed Shrike ♀

Starling

Hawfinch ♂

Greenfinch ♂

Goldfinch

Siskin ♂

**Linnet** *Acanthis cannabina* 13cm (5¼in) Male has chestnut back and grey head with, in summer, red crown and breast; female and young duller. All show white feather edgings in wing and tail. **Flight** Rapid, often wavering and dancing. **Voice** A rapid twittering call and pleasant song. **Habitat** Breeds in scrub thickets and hedgerows, spreads to a variety of open country in autumn and winter. **Distribution** Resident, breeding throughout Great Britain and Ireland.

**Twite** *Acanthis flavirostris* 13·5cm (5¼in) More tawny with heavier dark streaking than female and young Linnet, and an orange-buff face. In winter the bill is yellow. **Flight** Similar to Linnet. **Voice** Calls a nasal 'tsweet' and a Linnet-like twitter. **Habitat** Breeds in moorland and hill areas. Also shore, saltings and coastal fields in winter. **Distribution** Resident, breeding mainly in the west of Scotland and Ireland; locally elsewhere in Scotland and the Pennines. Regular in winter on the English coast between Lincoln and Sussex.

**Redpoll** *Acanthis flammea* 13cm (5in) Small, plump, feeding acrobatically in trees. Males differ from females in summer in having a pinkish breast and rump. **Flight** Light and often high. **Voice** Call a metallic twittering 'chuch-uch-uch'; trilling song sometimes given in a circular song flight. **Habitat** Mainly birch woods and conifers. **Distribution** Resident, breeding in most parts except central southern England, more widespread in winter.

**Bullfinch** *Pyrrhula pyrrhula* 14·5cm (5¾in) Both sexes are unmistakable. Young duller with brown cap. **Flight** Undulating; white rump clearly visible. **Voice** Call a soft piping 'peu'. **Habitat** Areas with plenty of thick cover. **Distribution** Resident in most areas.

**Crossbill** *Loxia curvirostra* 16·5cm (6½in) Crossed mandibles may be seen at close range. **Flight** Rapid and undulating; heavy head and forked tail visible. **Voice** A loud 'chip-chip', both in flight and when feeding. **Habitat** Coniferous woodland. **Distribution** Resident in the Highlands, parts of East Anglia, Hampshire and locally elsewhere. Following periodic eruptions may breed in many other areas.

**Chaffinch** *Fringilla coelebs* 15cm (6in) Our commonest finch. **Flight** Wing-bars and white outer tail feathers noticeable. **Voice** A loud 'pink'; in spring a clear 'whee', and a short, loud song accelerating to a final flourish. **Habitat** Varied, provided that bushes or trees are available for nesting. **Distribution** Resident, breeding throughout Great Britain and Ireland.

**Brambling** *Fringilla montifringilla* 14·5cm (5¾in) Sexes rather similar in winter. **Flight** Conspicuous white rump. **Voice** A metallic 'tsweek', or 'chuc-chuc-chuc'. **Habitat** Woods, especially beech, rough weedy areas, stubble, etc. **Distribution** Winter visitor to most parts.

Linnet

Twite

Redpoll

Bullfinch

Crossbill

Chaffinch

Brambling
winter

# Buntings family Emberizidae

**Corn Bunting** *Emberiza calandra* 18cm (7in) A plump, uniformly brown-streaked bird with a large bill. **Flight** Heavy often with legs dangling. **Voice** An abrupt, dry 'quit'; song ends with a sound like a small bunch of keys jangling. **Habitat** Open farmland, commons, waste land. **Distribution** Resident, breeding mainly in east coast counties; rather local in the west and in Ireland.

**Yellowhammer** *Emberiza citrinella* 16·5cm (6½in) Female and juvenile less yellow than the bright male. **Flight** Chestnut rump and white outer tail feathers conspicuous. **Voice** A metallic 'twink' call; song, commonly written 'a little bit of bread and no cheese', consists of a high-pitched series ending in a longer note. **Habitat** Farmland, hedgerow, heath, scrub, young plantations. **Distribution** Resident, breeding in all areas.

**Cirl Bunting** *Emberiza cirlus* 16·5cm (6½in) Male easily separated from Yellowhammer by bold patterning, females by their olive-brown, not chestnut, rump. **Flight** Rather dipping. **Voice** A thin 'zit'; song a brief metallic rattle on one note. **Habitat** Pasture and other open areas with trees, hedges, and scrub. **Distribution** Resident, breeding locally in south and south-west England.

**Reed Bunting** *Emberiza schoeniclus* 15cm (6in) Females and young are duller than male in breeding plumage, but have easily seen eye and moustachial stripes. **Flight** Rather jerky with white outer tail feathers. **Voice** A loud 'chink', and a short squeaky song. **Habitat** Mainly damp areas with plentiful cover, increasingly in drier areas such as farmland, rough waste, heath. **Distribution** Resident in all areas.

**Snow Bunting** *Plectrophenax nivalis* 16·5cm (6½in) Females much the same as a winter male, though less white on wings and tail. **Flight** Swift and undulating; white underparts and wing patches conspicuous. **Voice** Calls a rippling 'tiriririp' and a clear, ringing 'teu'. **Habitat** Breeds on barren mountain tops; winters on lower ground, often close to the coast. **Distribution** A few pairs breed in northern Scotland; otherwise a widespread winter visitor.

**House Sparrow** *Passer domesticus* 14·5cm (5¾in) Highly gregarious. **Flight** Rapid. **Voice** A loud 'chee-ip' and various chirps and twitters. **Habitat** Very varied but usually close to human habitation. **Distribution** Resident, breeding in all areas.

**Tree Sparrow** *Passer montanus* 14cm (5½in) Unlike more robust House, the sexes are similar. Note brown crown, black cheek spot. **Flight** More agile than House. **Voice** Various short calls including a high-pitched 'teck'. **Habitat** Typically woods and other areas with mature trees. Spreads to open land in winter. **Distribution** Resident, breeding in many areas though only locally in the west.

Corn Bunting

Yellowhammer
♂

Cirl Bunting
♂

Reed Bunting
♀
♂

Snow Bunting
winter
♂

Tree Sparrow

House Sparrow
♀
♂

# Index

Figures in italic
type refer to the species
description with
accompanying colour
illustration.